FINDING YOUR FUTURE

Books by Peter Shaw

Mirroring Jesus as Leader (Cambridge, Grove Books, 2003)

Conversation Matters: how to engage effectively with one another (London, Continuum Press, 2004)

The Four Vs of Leadership: vision, values, value-added, vitality (Chichester, Capstone, 2005)

Forthcoming books by Peter Shaw

Making Effective Use of Coaching, with Robin Linnecar (Chichester, Capstone, 2007)

Making Difficult Decisions (Chichester, Capstone, 2008)

FINDING YOUR FUTURE

The Second Time Around

PETER SHAW CB

DARTON · LONGMAN + TODD

The author's royalties are going to Tearfund, which provides practical help for those in poverty to enable them to have a future.

First published in 2006 by
Darton, Longman and Todd Ltd
1 Spencer Court
140–142 Wandsworth High Street
London SW18 4JJ

ISBN-10 0-232-52677-X
ISBN-13 978-0-232-52577-6

A catalogue record for this book is available from the British Library.

Designed and produced by Sandie Boccacci
Phototypeset in 11/15pt Apollo
Printed and bound in Great Britain by
Cromwell Press, Trowbridge, Wiltshire

Dedicated to my son Graham,
whose words, 'Pretend you are 21 again,'
were so influential when I was thinking about my own future.

CONTENTS

FOREWORD

It seems all of our lives have distinct phases. Periods of stability; periods of change. Our lives will be punctuated by significant, perhaps even overwhelming, events. We will all have changes of direction. Some help making sense of the choices and options, working out what to carry forward and what to leave behind, is very welcome.

Five years ago, after a career in increasingly large and complex international businesses, most recently as Managing Director of Coca-Cola Great Britain, I made the life-changing decision to leave the familiar world of the multinational and start up my own business, a food and drink company with the unlikely name of Big Thoughts Ltd. It was not an easy transition, with many key decisions to be made, but so far, I have been fortunate and it has been a successful venture.

At about the same time, I became a founding member of the Learning and Skills Council (LSC), a public body charged with ensuring that everyone in England has the skills they need both to fulfil their own potential and to help their organisations prosper. It was in this context that I first met and worked with Peter Shaw when he was a Director General at the Department for Education and Skills.

I quickly came to regard Peter as something of a mentor; a very perceptive and effective coach. His good counsel helped me with the transition into the public sector. Two years ago, I took advantage of the freedom of running my own business to devote a substantial proportion of my time to being Chair of the LSC. This is a huge task, but a real opportunity to help people prepare for the challenges ahead and have the confidence to tackle them.

A very large part of the remit of the LSC is to enable people to acquire the skills they need 'second time around', making sure that what they missed out on at school, they can catch up on as an adult. I have a particular interest in helping people learn new skills and approaches that will enable them to find and succeed in a decent job with good prospects. So I was intrigued by Peter's book and enjoyed the characteristically insightful, practical and highly readable text. I particularly like the checklists and prompts and am sure that many people will find them useful to reflect on at key decision times. I believe new beginnings are always possible even from seemingly difficult situations.

In a rapidly changing world, there is so much uncertainty. At times when life may seem confusing and lacking direction, Peter's book does not promise any easy answers, but it does provide welcome and much-needed support for those who are seeking to find their future.

Chris Banks CBE
Chair: Learning and Skills Council

INTRODUCTION

Finding your future is what 18-to-22 year-olds are supposed to do. For the rest of us, finding our future was something we tried to do once, but strangely, we seem to have to do it again, and again, and again!

As adults we assume we should have found our future and be living it. But what if we are bored, frustrated or down-hearted? Do we have to stand still? Sometimes it feels as if our only option is to stick where we are and to paper over the cracks. You have made your own bed, now sleep in it! Television, the internet and retail therapy are sometimes anaes-thetics that help us ignore the cracks and stop us moving on.

We don't want to settle for second best. We don't want to be continually frustrated or feel a sense of failure. We recognise our responsibilities to family and friends and are sensitive to the values that are important to us. Maybe a major event has happened which has forced us to re-examine our priorities. Perhaps there has been a bereavement, a job change or the loss of a job, or the children have left home. Perhaps we are becom-ing reconciled to being single. It is time to think back, reflect and move on. We want to find our future again. We are ready to reassess our lives. Well, at least some of the time we feel this way!

This book is for anybody between the ages of 22 and 92 who wants to think about their next steps. The book will provide you with a framework to help you make your decisions. Some will be minor adjustments while others may be big changes.

The book is divided into four Sections: 'Starting-points', 'Taking Stock', 'Looking Forward' and 'Moving On'.

- **'Starting-points'** will help you establish where you are now through looking at frustrations, failure, fears and fortitude.
- **'Taking Stock'** will enable you to reflect on the various influences upon you, especially family, friends and finance, as well as looking at what the fundamentals are for you.
- **'Looking Forward'** looks at the prerequisites for your next steps, which might include forgiveness, following your fascinations, engaging with the freedom available to you, and using fasting or self-denial.
- **'Moving On'** will encourage you to develop foresight, a clear focus and a sense of fun, as you look for the fulfilment that embraces what is important to you.

Do take time to reflect on these issues. Sometimes change hits us and we have to make quick decisions. Even then, creating some space to stand back and reflect is valuable. Often transitions take a longer time than we think. We learn more about ourselves and step forward more slowly than we might wish. But that is the moment when we need to make some decisions and find our future.

My aim has been to draw from the range of experiences I have seen in many people and to write something that is engaged and practical. Each chapter contains bullet lists which are designed to encourage the reader to reflect on their own circumstances and next steps.

The thinking in this book is embedded in my own Christian heritage but draws from a wide range of influences. The book is designed to help readers reach their own conclusions on what matters to them, whether or not faith is important to them. My objective is that you should come out of your immersion in this book encouraged and challenged with a greater understanding of yourself and the options available to you. I hope this book will also bring you lots of joy! If I can make you smile, I will be delighted. The book can either be read right through or each of the chapters can be read and reflected upon separately.

Strong influences upon me in putting together this book have been my family, my friends and the many people I have worked with, both in Government and now as an executive coach. I am very grateful to them all, and especially to Judy Smith (for her excellent typing), Claire Salkeld (for managing my diary), Liz Piercy (for her clarity as an editor) and Jill Kirby and Mairi Eastwood, who gave me thoughtful feedback on the text. My thanks also go to Chris Banks for his generosity in writing the Foreword.

Different parts of our lives flow from the different contexts in which we live. Blending those contexts together is what this book is all about. Different parts of this book were written in Godalming, London, Swaledale, Boston and Vermont. Experiences from each place have flowed into the writing. I am especially grateful to Frances for her calmness and companion-ship in each of these special places.

PETER SHAW
Godalming, May 2006

STARTING-POINTS

This section is about where we begin. The key requirement is that we are honest with ourselves. There are many different starting-points. Yours might be:

- seeing *failure* as a gift;
- living with your *fears*;
- coping with your *frustrations*;
- learning from your own *fortitude*.

It may be elements of each of these. As you read through each chapter, reflect on what are the starting-points for you. From each of these starting-points we will be looking at how we can build from where we are, for every cloud has its silver lining.

Reflect on how working through failures can give you new strengths; acknowledge and understand your fears; be honest about your frustrations and embed the learning from your own fortitude.

You are about to begin the rest of your life. You may have a much stronger base on which to build than you expect.

Chapter 1
FAILURE

" With the right attitude, all the problems in the world will not make you a failure. With the wrong mental attitude, all the help in the world will not make you a success. "

Warren Deaton

" Failure is as much a part of life as success is and by no means something in front of which one sits down and howls as though it is a scandal and a shame. "

J. Neville Ward

Is failure a curse or a blessing? Failure can be very painful and can put us through agonies. Failure can also create new beginnings and lead us to look at horizons we had never contemplated before. Failure is an essential part of the 'weft and warp' of life. If we never failed we would become arrogant, self-opinionated and insensitive. Maybe we should celebrate our failures rather than hide them.

See failure as a starting-point

I am writing this chapter in Swaledale, the most beautiful part of the Yorkshire Dales. It is early May and the trees are just beginning to burst into green. The trees have looked dead for months: all of a sudden spring is here and there is new life in the old trunks. The new leaves are fresh and bright with many different shades of green. As you walk through the valley there is a brightness and a joy. It is as if the whole valley is saying, 'We were dormant for a while, but we are back again as vibrant and lively as ever.' The winter will have resulted in some branches coming down in the wind, but the trees are growing new branches to replace the old.

It is impossible to ignore the new life of trees in the spring. Sometimes new life in people is just as obvious; sometimes it is more hidden. After a relationship that ends, for some people, all of a sudden, they break out of the bleakness and are renewing old friendships. For others, the change is slower and more imperceptible. But over time it is clear that new life has begun.

Be honest about the pain

What are the failures that pain you most? Perhaps they are not attaining

- *the exam results you felt you deserved (or your parents expected of you);*
- *the university place or training opportunity you had hoped for;*
- *the job or promotion you had worked for;*
- *the home you had hoped for;*
- *the space you had dreamed of;*
- *the children you had longed for;*
- *the reputation you had aspired to;*
- *the sport you wanted to excel in;*
- *the friendships you had hoped for.*

Be honest about the failures that pain you most:

- *list them out in a quiet moment;*
- *rank them in order of what has caused you the greatest pain;*
- *identify which of these are painful because of the expectations of others.*

For example, is there still a sense of failure because of the expectations of parents about your exam results or your higher or further education? Try to think of this sense of failure as your parents' problem and not your problem, caused by their expectations and not yours.

Set alongside each source of pain the good things that have happened, such as:

- *the benefits of the education and training you received;*
- *the job experience you have had;*
- *the home you live in;*
- *the good friends who are important to you;*
- *the family that you are part of;*
- *the fitness that you do have;*
- *the opportunity to nurture and enable others;*
- *the fulfilment that came through encouraging others.*

Sometimes the sense of failure can be all consuming, especially after redundancy, a broken marriage, the death of a close member of the family, or the worsening of a physical disability. We then struggle through a sense of failure that seems interminable. Setting the good things alongside these sources of pain can seem trite and uncaring. But as soon as it is just about bearable to list the good things alongside the pain, it is worth trying to draw them out and reflect on them.

For example:

- *alongside redundancy are the skills I learnt in the job;*
- *alongside a broken marriage is the greater understanding I have about myself;*
- *alongside death are the memories I share of that person; and*
- *alongside physical disability is the pleasure of watching fit young people running around.*

It is never easy to hold the good things alongside painful memories of failure, but it is an essential step at some point along the healing process.

After redundancy the sense of failure can make someone very difficult to live with, as the working through of painful emotions takes time. But chance conversations can produce a new optimism – a gentle flower that needs careful cultivating. After a life crisis, irrationality in the use of finance can be so damaging for close relationships, but even this settles down. In retrospect redundancy can open up the most unexpected new horizons.

View failure as a gift

However painful the failure, there is always some good coming out of it. If you look back on your life's pilgrimage, there will have been failures, but often positive changes have grown out of those failures. I intensely disliked the MSc I did in Traffic Engineering, but it helped focus my mind on what was the right thing to do next. When I coach people, I draw on my failures more than my so-called successes, as the most strongly embedded learning often comes through experiences that have been painful.

Maybe it is helpful to picture every cloud as having a silver lining. In a series of jobs, whenever we were going through crises, I would always say, 'What is the silver lining?' Amidst all the careful handling of difficult situations, it was important to spend a little while on the silver lining. What are the new opportunities now opening up? What was previously off the agenda and might now be on the agenda because of a crisis? A boss once commented that I always saw the positive side in everything. This was said with a touch of frustration, but it was also an acknowledgement that seeing the positive was essential to working effectively through any demanding situation.

When has failure for you been a gift? When has it closed one door and opened up new horizons? It might have been a failed relationship, a failed job, a failed interview or a sporting catastrophe! It is much easier to do this in retrospect than in current reality. When we reflect in retrospect and see the beneficial outcomes, it acts as a reminder that good things can come out of current failures.

Whenever we experience failure, however intense, if we view it as a gift, it can be transformed in our minds. If someone gives us a gift, there is a sense of expectation. We experience pleasure, almost regardless of the content of the package.

Think of a gift you recently received.

- *Why did you enjoy receiving it?*
- *Have you been able to use it effectively?*
- *Was there any learning for you connected with the gift?*

Even in the intensity of failure, if you see the failure as a gift, there is a sense of expectation about what you are learning through it:

- *How is it enabling you to grow in understanding of yourself and others?*
- *What is its place on your life's pilgrimage?*
- *How is it helping you to clarify the next steps in your decisions?*

Sometimes our failures prompt a complete change in direction. We are focused on one set of goals and aspirations. The shock of our failure sends us in a different direction. We go through a conversion experience, our own 'Damascus Road' experience. The apostle Paul had been single-mindedly persecuting the Christians. Dramatically, he saw God through different eyes on the Damascus Road, and became a Christian leader instead of a persecutor.

If there is a past failure that still rankles, maybe now is the time to 'slay the dragon'. Can you move on and put it behind you? Set alongside it the good things that have happened. Put the past failure in a box and send it away. Metaphorically throw it over the edge of a cliff and wait for it to shatter.

Can you think of a failure you would like to put in a box?

- *Be very precise about what the failure was.*
- *Imagine the box – its shape and look.*
- *Throw it as far as you can.*
- *Listen for the shatter.*
- *Repeat this exercise at regular intervals if necessary.*

If you are going through a failure, try to put it in a wider context. Is it a pain you have been through before?

- *How did you work through it then?*
- *What would be the good results if you could work through it now?*
- *What would 'resurrection' mean if you could come out on the other side?*
- *What is the learning that needs to take place?*
- *How would you be stronger?*

Moving on from apparent failure to success

The seed has to die and break open before the grain can grow. Some seed falls by the wayside and is eaten by the birds, or grows a bit and is choked by the weeds. Some of the seeds we sow appear to be wasted, but then the apparent failure can be followed by an abundant harvest.

We hate to fail, but it is essential for our self-awareness. We may have been frustrated by our failure in history at school, but that self-awareness reinforced the value of studying technology at the next stage.

When we fail, it is important to be clear what we need to work on. When we are told that we are not very convincing, we need to know what we need to focus our efforts on. I do a lot of preparation of people for interviews, where it is important to clarify the messages someone is trying to communicate. We do a mock interview at the start. I feed back what in their approach has worked for me and what has not worked. We ask:

- Had they answered the questions?
- Were the answers engaging: was there any sense of passion?
- Was the impact in what they said or the way they said it?
- Were the answers too long or too short?

The first thing I try to do is to affirm people. I always say what is good about their approach: that reinforces the respect and trust between us. Then, to do my job properly, I must be explicit about the potential failures: we then work through them thoroughly. When an individual has worked really hard to address their issues and turn apparent failure into a successful interview approach, we celebrate with a cup of coffee. When they get the job, it might even be a glass of wine!

Addressing failings head on is essential in an interview situation, as this can lead to a markedly changed approach. In any work situation it is a gross untidiness to ignore failure. For someone to think they are doing fine, when they obviously are not, is unfair to them, to their colleagues and to their customers. How we do it is important. When we have had our own failings in a work situation, the people we respect most are those who have been honest with us but have done it in a way which was affirming and focused. They have believed we could change and grow, that new life and resurrection is possible.

Addressing failings in relationships can be much more sensitive. When we feel stuck or badly adrift, with only a minuscule sense of hope, we can go into a spiral of depression. Holding onto that sense of the possibility of resurrection can make such a difference. Our children are our children for ever: we can never give up on loving them and encouraging them. Similarly, we may work with colleagues over a long period, so openness about past failings can be cathartic and can enable new beginnings. People are often taken aback by such openness and are willing to make a fresh start. In relationships that are failing, the key to success is being open about our own failings rather than castigating someone else for *their* failings.

Moving on to new beginnings

Five things to do when you are in the midst of failure:

- *See if you can spot the hint of light at the end of the tunnel.*
- *Remember the learning from past failures.*
- *Hold onto the learning that is coming through this failure.*
- *Believe that resurrection and new life do happen.*
- *Try to put boundaries around the failure to limit its contamination of other areas of your life.*

John's story

Failure, however painful, is the start of new beginnings, a starting-point for new directions. John felt a strong sense of failure when his business life fell apart and he was made redundant. He had had high aspirations and had been doing well; he expected to gain a series of promotions. He knew where he wanted to go and was on a golden pathway to success. But over time the golden pathway turned into a weary treadmill as the company hit rough times: he felt he was being used and exploited. He lost his optimism and his work became mere drudgery. He felt it was all a very hard grind and began to feel a strong sense of failure. He lost his enthusiasm at work and became a pain to live with. He was living a slow, painful death inside in terms of his self-worth.

At last John went through his own resurrection. What was he good at? Science and physics. What did he enjoy doing most? Talking about physics. What gave him special pleasure? Being with children and young people. John's resurrection came through training to be a science teacher. The training lifted his sights. Out of the depths of his sense of failure came a new beginning. In his mid forties, he began a new career in education.

> *" Far better it is to dare things, to win glorious triumphs, even though checkered by failure. "*
>
> Theodore Roosevelt

Chapter 2
FEAR

" No passion so effectively robs the mind of all its powers of acting and reasoning as fear. "

Edmund Burke

" Curiosity will conquer fear even more than bravery will. "

James Stephens

Living with our fears is part of life. Our fears are just there, sometimes greater and sometimes less. They are part of who we are. The strength of our fears will rise and fall: bringing fears under reasonable control is not always straightforward. Rubbing along living with our fears is a fact of life: but sometimes we can contain or even befriend our fears.

What are your main fears? What keeps you awake at four o'clock in the morning? What do you worry about at work? What do you worry about most in terms of your family? I hope this chapter will enable you to address some of your fears and move on from them.

Be frank about the fears that you most worry about.

- *Write them down.*
- *Score them on a scale of 1 to 10, where 1 is illusory and 10 is highly likely.*
- *When is each fear at its worst?*

- *What are the warning signs that this fear might burst out?*
- *What in the past has reduced the size of the fear?*

Fear can be a good thing

My mother used to tell the story of how she ran faster than ever before when she saw a bull beginning to chase her in a field in the Yorkshire Dales. The adrenalin flowed and she ran fast to a wall and heaved herself over it before the bull could reach her. Fear got her out of difficulty. The fear of traffic makes us rightly cautious on busy roads, with measured fear keeping us safe in many different circumstances. William Cowper wrote the wise words, 'He has no hope who never had a fear.' Fear can be a driver for good, up to a point!

Beware of the damage that fear can bring

Have you ever been frozen in fear or caught in its headlights? Unable to move, we become gripped by fear and paralysed. Two of my worst moments of fear involved my daughter. When she was two and we were in a department store in Worthing, we lost her. Panic rose in us: we rushed around searching for her; a message went out on the tannoy. Eventually we discovered her playing happily. Such relief after the panic of fear!

When my daughter was seven she went for ride on a round-about at a fair. We thought it was a roundabout that travelled horizontally, but it soon began to move vertically as well. I was paralysed with fear and couldn't wait for the ride to stop. My daughter did not particularly enjoy the ride but it was me who was struck with fear.

These moments can still sometimes give me mild nightmares but they also taught me that fear is part of life. As a parent you have to let go and accept that there are going to be moments of fear and moments of great joy.

Fear can be greatly overrated. Most of our worst fears never ever happen. In his book *The Gathering Storm*, Winston Churchill wrote about the early days of the Second World War: 'When I look back on all those worries, I remember the story of the old man who said on his deathbed that he had had a lot of trouble in his life, most of which had never happened.'

Fear can be very damaging. When it gnaws inside us like a cancer, it grows and eats up our hope and joy. Sheila Delaney wrote, 'I am not frightened of the darkness outside. It's the darkness inside the houses that I don't like.' Bottling up our fears can be like creating an unexploded bomb inside us.

It can be helpful to look back and write down:

- *What have been the moments of your greatest fear?*
- *How did you react and cope in those moments?*
- *How many of those fears have been real and how many have turned out to be not nearly as bad as you had anticipated?*
- *Did any good come out of those moments of fear?*

Perfect love drives out fear

There is a fascinating interrelationship between love and fear. The apostle John wrote, 'There is no fear in love. Perfect love drives out fear.' As we reinforce the bonds of love, fear will diminish. For example, the more we love our children and let them go, the less we will fear for their welfare. Recently our eldest son was leading a building project for a charity in the slums of Nairobi, our youngest son was teaching English as a foreign language in China and our daughter was in Luton, which appeared to be the most dangerous of the three places, as bombs were discovered in a parked car in the town. We had apprehensions but we focused on our love for our children as a way of driving out those apprehensions and fears. It seemed to work, aided by the occasional email.

Understanding our fears

Addressing our fears is not about ignoring them; it is about defining them and understanding them. Looking at a fear from a variety of angles can help us to understand it and contain it.

If you wake fearful at 4 a.m.:

- *be explicit about what the fear is;*
- *perhaps write it down, with three reasons why the fear is there;*
- *three ways in which the fear could be addressed;*
- *three reasons why it is not as acute as it might at first appear.*

Later in the day, take another look at the notes you made.

- *Are the reasons for the fear still there?*
- *Has the fear increased or diminished during the day?*
- *Have you been able to apply any of the ways to address the fear?*
- *Are there practical steps you can take to reduce the fear further?*

Living with the fear of the unknown

Often we take a decision not knowing what the eventual outcome will be. We step out, believing we are doing the right thing. Members of a village church recently decided to build an extension to include two rooms which would be used for a wide range of community activities involving ... disabled people and the elderly. They raised a amount of money initially but were apprehensive a... next steps. Could they raise the balance of the money needed when they had already committed a significant amount themselves? They talked about holding fast to the path which they had set themselves. They reflected on what the word 'courageous' meant. They talked about the words of Martin Luther King, 'Courage faces fear and thereby masters it.' They spent some time visualising all those people who would be using the facilities. The more they upheld these people in their minds, the more their fears about the project began to diminish.

Entering the unknown is both worrying and exciting at the same time. Trying to focus on the newness of the previously unknown in order to minimise the fear is a powerful way of beginning to move on. We tend to focus on the scary aspects of the unknown, but thinking about its positive elements can be such an encouragement, enabling us to be excited about something new.

Living through a fear of failure

The fear of failure is a powerful force for good or ill. It is a big motivator: it ensures that people get things done. On the other hand, the fear of not being able to pay the mortgage or not having enough resources to live on can gnaw away at our strength. The fear of poor health or unemployment can drain us of energy and whittle away our enthusiasm and optimism. Marie Curie wrote, 'Nothing in life is to be feared, it is only to be understood. Now is the time to understand more so that we may fear less.' Understanding involves acknowledging our fears and trying to contain them.

A key way of coping with our fear of failure is to talk about it with our family and friends. A trusted friend whom we love dearly can help us talk about our fears. It is through being embraced in good friendship that we can move on from being mesmerised by the fear of failure. A colleague once shared with me the phrase, 'Love is the only reality: fear is unreal.' On the surface, this seemed a bit trite. But more than once I have used that phrase, and it has had an important impact. As individuals have focused on the people with whom they share their greatest affection, their fears have begun to become less and less real.

Reflect on these words: 'Love is the only reality: fear is unreal.'

- *With whom is love so important?*
- *How does the permanence of that love support you?*
- *Does reflecting on the love of those around you help you drive out fear?*

Living through the fear of change

A few years ago I switched jobs: I ceased to be a Director General with large numbers of staff and became an executive coach. It was a fulfilling transition which I wanted to make. I was a bit fearful, but in my emotions I moved on from my previous world within about four days and relished my second career. The fear disappeared very quickly: the change for me had been a powerful force for good.

When I was writing this chapter in Godalming, all three of our youngsters were departing for university, which meant a major lifestyle change for Frances and I. We have been trying to look at it positively: we planned a number of weekends either away or doing specific activities at home. We will miss our kids greatly but there is an excitement about the changes too. John Henry Newman wrote, 'Fear not that your life shall come to an end, but rather fear that it shall never have a beginning.' Even though we are apprehensive about change, it brings a richness. How dull life would be if there was no opportunity for change.

Getting our fears in proportion

Being curious about our fears can help to conquer them. We should think of fear as inevitable but controllable.

What practical steps can you take to get your fear into proportion? They might be:

- *talking to close family members;*
- *sharing with close friends;*
- *doing something very different, like walking, swimming, or reading a novel;*
- *moving completely away from the context that causes the fear; or*
- *being deliberately in the place which causes the fear, and controlling it;*
- *thinking of those whose fear is far more acute than your own.*

When Mary, the mother of Jesus, and Mary Magdalene found the tomb empty after Jesus' crucifixion, they hurried to the disciples, 'afraid yet filled with joy'. For these two women fear and joy were intermingled. When we go through change we are often 'afraid yet filled with joy'.

Beware the fear of success

Nelson Mandela, in his inaugural speech in 1994, talked of the fear of success. Quoting Marianne Williamson, he said, 'Our deepest fear is not that we are inadequate. Our deepest fear is that we are powerful beyond measure. It is our light, not our darkness that most frightens us.'

We can be fearful about challenges that new opportunities will bring: fearful that what we are striving for will actually happen. If we are successful, we will have to make important decisions, or teach a classroom full of children, or perform surgical operations, or give advice at the Citizens' Advice Bureau. When we are fearful about our responsibilities, it can help to reflect on the work that went into creating those opportunities, alongside the joy we can bring to others through these new responsibilities.

Moving on to new beginnings

Five things to do when you are in the midst of fear:

- *try to understand the causes of the fear;*
- *try to be as rational as possible in the way you respond;*
- *remember that many fears are illusory;*
- *embrace in your mind those you love;*
- *gradually try to reduce the size of the fear.*

Mary's story

Mary hated working for her boss. He was aggressive and demanding, and she was afraid of his words and his anger. This fear had eaten into the rest of her life, and consequently she had become fearful of a wide range of people and situations. She kept looking down rather than up: the fear got to her, sapped her energy, killed her confidence.

She was signed off by her doctor with depression. She felt humiliated and couldn't face work again. It was her ten-year-old daughter who loved her back to health. She looked after her mother with lots of drinks, stories and hugs. She got her to draw a picture of her favourite scenery. A few weeks later her daughter asked her to draw the same scene again. She knew that her mum was getting better because on the second occasion she drew the scenery and then put cows in the field. They then began to talk about what the cows were doing. A playfulness and joy had returned. The perfect love of the daughter had driven out the fear in the mother. Her favourite scene now included new life and energy. It was no longer a static picture but was full of cheerfulness.

> *" Nothing in the affairs of men is worthy of great anxiety. "*
>
> Plato

Chapter 3
FRUSTRATION

" Absence from whom we love is worse than death, and frustrated hope severer than despair. "

William Cowper

" Much of our activity these days is nothing more than a cheap anaesthetic to deaden the pain of an empty life. "

Richard Foster

Is frustration a good thing or a bad thing? It can gnaw away at our sense of well-being. It can make us angry, irritable and depressed. But understanding our frustrations can lead us to a new understanding of ourselves. It can draw us to a greater sense of purpose and determination to make a difference in those areas that are most important to us. Taking a detached look at our frustrations can help us to be much clearer about our priorities.

Define your frustrations

In this chapter we will think about putting our frustrations into proportion – looking at why they happen and how we can deal with them. We will then look at how frustrations can be used as a spur to assess where we are – how they can be a power for good and how we can move on from them.

Frustrations come in many shapes and sizes. This is a very trivial example but one that typifies Saturday morning frustration after a busy week. One Saturday I decided to have my hair cut and went to visit a barber in a nearby small town. The blind was down and in the window was a small notice saying, 'On holiday until next Tuesday'. I felt mild frustration as John is an excellent barber, we always have a good conversation and he charges a reasonable rate. I was determined to get my hair cut but the next place I arrived at was busy.

I tried a third barber's shop where the queue was fairly short. This was a modern place with loud music and trendy furniture. All three barbers were generously covered in tattoos and were taking leisurely breaks between each customer. I was getting more and more frustrated by the noise and the delay. Eventually my turn came and my frustration began to ease. I saw another side of these trendy young barbers when they talked about raising money for the Save the Children fund by charging a reduced rate over a 24-hour period, with all the money going to charity. My frustration had blinded me to the essential goodness of what they were trying to do. I left the shop with an excellent haircut and felt chastened.

What causes your frustrations? Is it frustration with yourself or others? Frustrations come at many different levels, from blockages in our career to the barber's shop being shut.

What have been your biggest frustrations this week?

- *List them out and rank them in order of importance.*
- *Which of them have been frustrations with somebody else?*
- *Which of them have been frustrations with yourself?*

For each frustration:

What has caused you to be wound up?
What has helped you move on from the frustration?
What has helped you get that frustration in proportion?

Have any of the following helped in overcoming the frustration?

- *Laughing at yourself.*
- *A side-comment from a friend who has seen the funny side of what is happening.*
- *A recognition that the frustration is relatively unimportant.*
- *A new piece of information entering your mind. (For example, buying a newspaper from the newsagent next door to the shut barber's shop helped me move on from the initial frustration.)*
- *Was there a sense of this particular incident mattering much less than you had initially thought?*

If you look at your main frustrations over, say, the last couple of years:

- *Can you define those frustrations?*
- *How angry did they make you feel?*
- *For how long did those frustrations 'eat at your soul'?*
- *What helped you to begin to move on from those frustrations?*
- *What did you learn through those frustrations?*

Our frustrations have many different causes. They might result from:

- *the expectations of our parents;*
- *our own strong sense of ambition and wanting to make a difference;*

- unpredictable external factors that have thrown us off course;
- the behaviour of others who are doing things that are not on our agenda;
- the irrational behaviour of our colleagues;
- the behaviour of the children in our lives, who are continually stretching the boundaries;
- a lack of personal fulfilment.

Looking carefully at the causes of your frustrations can help to get them in proportion:

- If the frustration comes from the expectation of others, it is, to an extent, their problem and not yours.
- If the frustration comes from the behaviour of your colleagues, some understanding of the pressures they are under can help you to get the frustration in proportion.
- If the frustration comes from the persistent activity of the children in your life, be thankful for their energy.
- If the frustration comes from being very cross with yourself, maybe there are some key questions about your own perspective that ought to be addressed.

When you are feeling frustrated, the first question to ask is, 'Why is it happening?' The second question is, 'How do I keep the frustration under control so that it does not damage other people?' The heart of dealing with a frustration is to try and understand where it has come from and then to look at its impact on you.

To what extent is the frustration:

- a stimulus to make changes in a positive way?

- *leading you down blind alleys?*
- *eroding your self-confidence?*
- *damaging the relationships that are most important to you?*

When are your frustrations at their worst? Is there something about the time of day, the time of the month, what you have eaten, the people with whom you have been talking, or your sleeping pattern? Understanding when and how the frustrations are at their worst is the first step in moving on from them.

What have you learnt through frustration?

To help get your current frustrations in proportion, it is well worth looking back at what particularly frustrated you as a teenager. What made you really cross when you were 16? How did you cope with that anger? When were you able to move on from that feeling of lack of worth? What released you from the frustration? Were there cathartic moments when the sense of frustration was replaced by joy? It might have been the quality of friendship with your peers that helped make the difference.

On Tuesday evenings, 30 young people will often gather at our house. They squash into the back room after a day at the local secondary schools or sixth form college. They come often tired and frustrated, and they unwind by chatting, drinking squash and eating biscuits. After an hour they go into study groups, putting the world to rights and talking about their frustrations, their joys and the week ahead. In this informal setting they move on from their frustrations. There is a powerful sense of mutual support as all that wonderful energy is changed from frustration into a sharing, positive outlook. The way that the transformation can happen so quickly from tiredness and frustration into energy and laughter is a wonderful example of how we can bounce back if we let ourselves be supported and cheered by others.

What are our frustrations telling us?

Looking objectively at our frustrations can be a very salutary experience:

- *If you are very frustrated by your job, maybe it is time to have a serious conversation with your boss about the structure of the job.*
- *If the frustration is based on aspects of the work which are not easily changeable, maybe it is time to think about moving on.*
- *If moving on is not an option, how can the frustration be limited both in the design of the work and also in ensuring that there are sources of joy in other aspects of your life?*
- *If the frustration is with those closest to you, is it time to have a heart-to-heart?*
- *If the frustration is because of wider pressures of expectation from those in your community, is it time to begin to prioritise some of those commitments and be ready to say a firm 'No'?*
- *If the frustration comes from a lack of sleep, is it time to change the pattern of your day or your week?*

How can your frustrations be eased?

Sometimes help to put our frustrations in proportion can come through unexpected ways. Linda is wheelchair-bound with a chronic form of MS. For many years she taught midwifery and was skilled and energetic in her work. Her lively approach was such an encouragement to her students. It is now sometimes difficult to hear and understand her words. She must get frustrated with the limitations on her physical powers, but there is a calmness and resolve in her. She will sometimes read a lesson or contribute some of the prayers at our church, which is a living community to which she belongs. Listening to her quiet words, spoken with difficulty, puts my frustrations into a completely different perspective. Watching Linda cope with her frustrations in such a calm and measured way is a tribute to her resolve and a message to those around her that our frustrations are mild in comparison.

Have you ever watched the frustration of a toddler trying to walk or to catch one of their friends? The bouncing energy turns into tears so easily. This mixture of excitement and then utter frustration is a microcosm of what we often experience. We then see the youngsters bounce back, and the tears are wiped away and they are running around the garden again. The oscillation from frustration to joy is so fast for the toddler. Sometimes it feels much slower for us. Frustration can seem interminable, but it can end and we can move on.

Being frustrated by unfairness

We can feel very uptight if we believe that we have been treated unfairly. It is particularly acute when an organisation stresses the importance of fairness and clearly fails to live up to those standards: a common feeling for anyone working in large organisations! That sense of unfairness can eat away at our well-being. Sometimes the best antidote is a generous heart. How generous are you to the person who has been promoted much more quickly than you were, or whose wages have just had a big increase? How generous are we in our hearts to those who seem to have had an easier life?

Being frustrated by unfairness can be a very powerful driver. It was this frustration that led Wilberforce in his drive to end slavery. It is also a big driver for those putting a lot of energy into fair trade or reducing world poverty. Our frustrations can be a huge source of power for good.

How can your frustrations be a power for good?

- *What might they be telling you about your future priorities?*
- *What might they be telling you about the gifts you have that could be used in different ways?*
- *Does it mean that now is the time to change direction?*
- *Is it time to change the way you show your love to those closest to you?*

Sometimes our frustrations have to be addressed head on, but sometimes it is best to walk away from them. The wisdom we need is to distinguish which is the right course of action! A key starting-point is a sense of what is alterable and what isn't. Looking through the eyes of others can help put our frustrations into a different perspective as we talk them through with friends and colleagues.

At the heart of moving on from frustrations is as clear an understanding as possible about where they come from, the belief that there are always things to learn from frustrations, and a strong sense that out of frustration can come a new resolve and a greater sense of hope for the future.

Moving on to new beginnings

Five things to do when you are in the midst of frustration:

- *Remember how you have coped with past frustrations.*
- *Set the current frustration alongside current joys.*
- *Try to accept that some frustrations will be there for ever.*
- *Imagine different ways in which you could move on from particular frustrations.*
- *Be courageous in thinking of actions you might take.*

Helen's story

Helen has worked her way up in a national organisation. She is concerned that she isn't rising as fast as some of her colleagues, although to the wider world she looks successful. For the last ten years there has been a persistent health problem which has been recently diagnosed as mild Parkinson's Disease. It is a great relief to know what the issue is: this means she can plan ahead more effectively, knowing the likely pathway for the disease.

Helen can begin to accept why sometimes her vision is blurred and why movement can be difficult. She has begun to accept that her health is better at different times of day and has a measured plan of how to cope. She is building into her month special times with her husband, lots of visits to the theatre and cinema, and weekends away. She is making the best use of the organisation's introduction of a nine-day fortnight, involving working hard and sometimes long hours on nine days, with the reward of a long weekend every fortnight.

The frustration caused by the health issue will not go away. But she is controlling it and working through it and not letting it erode her natural cheerfulness and sense of joy. She is remarkably confident in her approach to life and philosophical about what the future holds. Those around her are often more worried than she is, as she has learnt to live with her frustrations to a remarkable degree.

> *" True hope is swift, and flies with a swallow's wings; kings it makes gods, and meaner creatures kings. "*
>
> William Shakespeare

Chapter 4
FORTITUDE

" But welcome fortitude, and patient cheer,
And frequent sights of what is to be borne!
Such sights, or worse as are before me here –
Not without hope we suffer and we mourn. "

William Wordsworth

" She could bear the disappointment of other people
with tolerable fortitude. "

Charles Dickens

Does 'fortitude' seem a rather dated word? The *Oxford English Dictionary* defines it as 'Moral strength or courage: firmness in the endurance of pain or adversity'. Fortitude is about how we cope in times of emptiness, sadness or grief. It is how we work through times of dullness and false dawns in different aspects of our lives. Maybe our fortitude is much greater than we think it is and can provide a sure foundation for the future.

What have been your desert places?
We all go through desert places where the dryness never seems to end. The environment doesn't seem to change, the horizon gets no closer and the sand gets in our eyes. The wind is in our faces and not pushing us forward from behind. Each

step is a trudge, there is a perpetual tiredness and often an emptiness.

Reflect on:

- *What have been your desert places?*
- *What has been your equivalent of the never-changing horizon, the lack of variety in the environment and the biting wind?*
- *What has been the hardest thing to cope with in the desert places?*
- *What has kept you going? What have been the glimpses of the oasis that you have kept in your mind?*
- *What have been the characteristics of that inner courage that has kept you going?*
- *Who have been your companions who have encouraged you?*
- *Who has provided the water-bottle and given you hospitality on the way?*

As you reflect on the different desert places you have been through:

- *Do you find them more or less easy to cope with?*
- *What has been the type of oasis that has helped you most?*
- *Are you able to conserve your water and use it more effectively?*
- *Does each desert place slightly prepare you for the next one?*

As you look to the future, what types of desert places do you see? Are they principally about:

- *your current work situation as economic circumstances change?*

- *your current family situation as the children grow older?*
- *your place in the community where you are faced with conflicting priorities?*

Fortitude through sadness and grief

Sadness and grief keep changing their shape at different phases of life. For the child there is the sadness at the end of the birthday party or the grief when the guinea-pig dies. In the teenage years it is a sadness of broken friendships and perhaps the grief of a grandparent dying. In the middle years it is the sadness of children leaving home or the grief of parents dying. In later years grief hits us as our friends die. At any age we can be 'cut to the quick' by sadness that leaves us heartbroken. Thankfully, we never become immune to grief. When a loved one dies, the grieving process can take us a couple of years and pain can seem never-ending.

Fortitude when there is sadness or grief is not about blanking out the pain. It is about celebrating the lost loved one and being ready to move on. In the Hindu tradition there is a lovely practice of giving new clothes to those closest to someone who has died as a mark of moving on and a new beginning. Fortitude is about cherishing the memory of those we love and then moving on. It is about giving full flow to the tears and quietly building the resolve to continue living with a strong sense of purpose.

When was your strongest moment of fortitude in the face of sadness or grief? Was it:

- *the death of a loved one?*
- *a broken friendship?*

- *a career that disappeared?*
- *a tragedy in your community?*

What helped nurture your fortitude in these situations:

- *your sense of purpose?*
- *your friends and family?*
- *your previous experience?*
- *your faith in a God who upholds you?*
- *your inner resolve?*
- *memories of those you loved?*
- *the companionship of colleagues?*

Living through tough work situations

All of us who have worked for a living or in a voluntary organisation will know of tough situations. You may have felt let down or even abused; you may have felt like a pawn in a bigger game where fairness and respect have gone out of the window. Fortitude is about maintaining your dignity in these difficult situations: it is about continuing to show a generosity of spirit while not letting your integrity be bullied.

Perhaps you have trusted someone to do a good job or trusted them with your good will. They have then let you down and you have had to take the flak: perhaps not immediately, because your organisation has said it believes in a 'no blame culture'. But perhaps a little later you are sidelined, and you feel aggrieved and cross. That sense of being 'hard done by' stays with you and can turn into resentfulness. This situation is all too frequent, even though you might not want to talk about it.

How to cope with resentfulness:

- *Try and define how it has happened and be very rational about its causes.*
- *Talk it out with a close friend.*
- *Try and accept that 'that's life'.*
- *Try to work through what are the best ways of moving on and leaving the resentfulness behind.*

Coping with false dawns

There is nothing more depressing than a mirage. There seems to be a lake ahead: we rush towards it, our spirits rise, but the lake is just a reflection. We stand still, not understanding what has happened, and our shoulders and spirits droop. It is right to keep looking for signs of hope: the chink that shows that there is a world outside. False dawns can keep us going, but living through them uses up our resources of courage.

What have been the false dawns that you have had to cope with?

- *Is there a pattern about them?*
- *Have they, to some extent, helped you to move on and be realistic?*
- *Can you recognise when they might be coming?*

Sometimes words of encouragement that are spoken to us, especially at performance reviews, can paint a falsely rosy picture. The words are intended to motivate, and they do to some extent. But the building up of false expectations is one of the most damaging things that any boss can do. Unrealistic expectations lead to disappointment, resentment and even bitterness.

Think of those people who have been responsible for creating false dawns in you. If you can explicitly forgive them for that misrepresentation, then you can more easily move on from the resentment that a false dawn might have created in you.

How to cope with false dawns:

- *Look back on previous experiences that have helped you come through false dawns.*
- *Hold on to a strong sense of reality.*
- *Enjoy the love of those around you.*
- *Feel confident that you are a step closer to the horizon, however far away it is.*

Do patience and persistence help?

We have pictures in our minds of enormous patience and persistence. It might be the children of Israel in the Sinai Desert, or Solzhenitsyn in a Russian prison, or Terry Waite in solitary confinement, or Nelson Mandela resolved to end apartheid. Great people full of patience and persistence sometimes seem unreal and superhuman.

Patience and persistence are not just for the great and the good. The patience of the carer for a mentally handicapped child or the persistence of the single mum raising a family on a small income are examples that are around us all the time. We can surprise ourselves by our own patience and persistence. As we look back, there is often more fortitude that has flowed through patience and persistence than we recognise.

Celebrating small successes

When things are tough, small celebrations are all the more

important. We celebrate each minor development of a young child. The first step or the first word are broadcast to all our friends, and yet we hardly ever celebrate coping steadily with difficult situations. We can celebrate small successes in working through tough situations with just a cup of tea in a special cup, or a chocolate biscuit, or some long deep breaths. We avoid celebrating at our peril: the power of the short celebration can raise our spirits and keep up that fortitude.

Can you celebrate:

- *the completion of something you found difficult?*
- *getting through a tough day at work?*
- *reaching a milestone towards a long-term aspiration?*
- *the breaking of a persistent behaviour that has been unhelpful?*

Celebrating major milestones is even more important! When Frances and I celebrated our thirtieth wedding anniversary, our three children devised an orienteering course for the two of us. It demanded a lot of patience (to try and understand the instructions) and even more persistence (we were required to walk a very long way). But what joy it was to celebrate 24 years of parenthood. Maybe the patience and persistence we had to show in the orienteering walk were a reflection of patience and persistence over 24 years with three wonderful children.

The woman who had ten silver coins and lost one, lit a lamp, swept the house and searched carefully until she found it. When she found the lost coin she called her friends and neighbours together and said, 'Rejoice with me; I have found my lost coin!' She was persistent until she found it and then celebrated. Her fortitude was about persistence and then sharing and celebrating together.

How can you best celebrate:

- *at the end of the week?*
- *at the end of this month?*
- *at the end of this year?*

Accepting the generosity of others

When you go through tough periods, one of the most difficult things to do is to accept the generosity of others. The tougher it is, the more independent we feel we have to be. The tougher the situation, the less we might want to talk about it or share it. Maybe it is in those situations when we need the generosity of others most. Accepting the generosity of hospitality, cheerfulness and listening is accepting a priceless gift. Being ready to accept with open arms is not a denial of our fortitude, it is part of the way our fortitude is preserved and nurtured.

It might be worth reflecting on:

- *Who has been particularly generous to you?*
- *In what way was this generosity shown?*
- *How willingly did you accept this generosity?*
- *How good were you at saying thank you?*

Moving on to new beginnings

Five things to do when your fortitude begins to falter:

- *Remember how far you have travelled.*
- *Give thanks for the patience and persistence that have been*

part of your journey so far.

- *Give thanks for all of those who have upheld you.*
- *Think of what you can celebrate.*
- *Decide who you can share that celebration with.*

Rachel's story

Now well into their seventies, Rachel and her husband Ron had moved into a smaller house. Ron's health was beginning to go: his heart was weak and his memory was not what it used to be. Gradually he began to fade, but was cheerful until the end. He died peacefully, leaving many good memories and special friends.

There were tears, but Rachel was clear that life must go on. She built a new life for herself based around good friends, her family and her church. She loved being with her grand-children, who gave her tremendous pleasure. Her cheerfulness was not superficial chatter but a deeply rooted acceptance of her new life. Her fortitude had kept her going but had also opened up new horizons. She was a joy to be with, as she had a rich gift of friendship, a strong faith and a positive outlook. She was above all an encourager. Although the pain of separation was there, it never seemed to intrude. She was full of good memories but was always engaged with the realities of day-to-day life. The future was still good, even at the age of 82.

> *" Courage is not simply one of the virtues, but the form of virtue at the testing point, which means at the point of highest reality. "*
>
> C. S. Lewis

Section B
TAKING STOCK

This section is about looking at some of the wider influences on you and considering their impact. When you take stock, there are likely to be many issues that flood into your mind. Perhaps some of the most important themes are:

- the influence of your *family* background and current family situation;
- the importance of your *friends*;
- constraints and options about *finance*;
- the *fundamentals* that are most important to you.

These elements can provide a framework for taking stock about where you have come from and what is important to you for the future.

To what extent do family and friends provide a foundation for the future? How important is finance to you? What are the fundamentals on which you most want to build?

You will move on from this section being clearer about what is important to you for the future. Through looking at the impact of family, friends and finance you will be firmer in your own mind about what are the fundamentals that matter to you most.

Chapter 5

FAMILY

" Treasure your families – the future of humanity passes by way of the family. "

Pope John Paul II

" Father and mothers, if you have children they must come first. Your success as a family, our success as a society, depends not on what happens in the White House, but on what happens inside your house. "

Barbara Bush

Where does your family fit in, both the family in which you grew up and the family which you are now part of? Our families can be the cause of such anguish and joy. Whether we like it or not, we are our parents' offspring and we have been powerfully influenced by them. Our impact on our own family and our wider family will be profound, whether we like it or not. Being absolutely clear about what we draw from our roots and how we want to move on in relation to our family is a crucial building-block for the future.

Understanding your family background

My father was brought up in Blackburn, where his father worked in a cotton mill. After the early death of his father, he had to leave school at the age of 12 and began work in an office. He made a successful career in accountancy although he was never qualified professionally. His first wife died of TB during the Second World War. A couple of years later he married his first wife's cousin, who was 20 years his junior. I was their one child and he died when I was seven.

My parents bequeathed me a determination and a single-mindedness for which I have always been grateful. Sometimes I have been too single-minded for my own good and too trusting of others. The oscillations in my work, both paid and unpaid, have reinforced in me how indebted I am to my parents for what keeps me going, while being equally conscious of some of the blinkering that has come from my family background.

In my work as a coach it is clear that the two dominant influences on individuals are their parents and their cultural background. These are often helpful pieces of information to know early on in a coaching relationship, because they give an immediate understanding of where an individual is likely to be coming from. Sometimes I decide deliberately not to seek out this information because it might condition my perspective about somebody at too early a stage.

Some of the most intriguing people come from mixed cultural backgrounds. Simon has a Moroccan father and a French mother, and as a child he was immersed in both the French and the Moroccan cultures. He has the gentleness and thoughtfulness of his mother and the expressiveness and liveliness of his father. This blend enables him to sit comfortably in the European and Middle Eastern cultures, treasuring his joint heritage. It also means that he sometimes feels disorientated – a stranger in each culture.

Reflect on the influence of your parents. In what ways are you like them? For example:

- *What do you treasure most about your background?*
- *What two or three things do you most appreciate about what your parents did for you?*
- *What characteristics of you are directly mirroring your parents?*
- *In what ways has the influence of your parents been a power for good on you?*
- *In what ways has the influence of your parents had downsides for you?*

A frequent problem is that we put a lot of pressure on ourselves to live up to our parents' expectations – spoken or unspoken. We lose the benefit of having people around us who love us unconditionally. Anna was working through some issues about the impact of her parents upon her. I asked, 'Do you let your parents love you enough?' She was very reflective. A week later she had a long heart-to-heart with her parents which took them into a new depth of relationship. There had been a barrier there: she had been trying to prove herself to her parents too much. Now there was an openness and a warm embrace without conditions, and the relationship moved into a new special phase which was much warmer and accepting.

Coping with guilt

Sometimes the ambitions our parents had for us produce considerable guilt if we do not fulfil what we believe are their aspirations for us. The best antidote can be talking this through with your parents. In the great majority of cases it will be abundantly clear that they love you as you are and not because of your success. Guilt can be so strong when we feel we have let people down, especially when it is our parents we are focusing on.

When there is anger in a family we feel upset. It can help to view the anger as the problem of others and not yours. In one family I know well, when the father remarried, a daughter from the original marriage became very unhappy and cut herself off from her stepmother after her father died. The step-mother could never understand what had happened and felt a burden of guilt. The breach was never healed and it took this lady a long time to accept that this was just how it was and that it was not worth worrying about it any more. It is a painful truth that you cannot solve every problem.

Moving on from family background

The toddler is moving away from his parents as he runs around in the garden, but he is soon back for a cuddle when he has fallen over. That moving away into wider and wider spheres increases at each stage and never ends. Just as there is a rich-ness in celebrating our similarities with our parents, there is also a richness in celebrating our differences.

Such as:

- *How do I want to push the boundaries even more than my parents did?*
- *How do I want to ensure a wider set of experiences than my parents were able to enjoy?*
- *How can I stretch my horizons beyond my background in terms of awareness of the wider world and a greater diversity of cultural perspectives?*

This is not about denying parenthood but about building on it and enriching it.

Creating new families

Time with children is fully absorbing. The best antidote to a demanding job is bouncing around with the children at the weekend. But we need to watch the danger that in aspiring for our children to do well we can so easily do damage.

Some of the most important questions when bringing up children must be:

- *Do we 'treasure the moment' enough with our children at special times?*
- *Do we show love enough in the way we are present and fully engaged with them?*
- *Are we too concerned about the future at the expense of the present?*
- *Do we celebrate enough when they are lively, argumentative and difficult? For within this energy are the seeds of their independence for the future.*
- *Are we worried enough when a child is too placid and pliable?*

If you are in a very busy job, it is easy to feel guilty about the limitations on the time you spend with your children. Sometimes the answer is to move into a different type of work, but often that isn't possible.

The solution may be around:

- *Focusing the time spent with your children in a more effective way.*

- *Having one-on-one time with individual children where they have your sole undivided attention.*
- *Devising 'mini expeditions'.*
- *Creating an element of surprise.*
- *Celebrating the rebellious moment (be it the stud in the ear or the tattoo on the calf).*

Perhaps the most difficult years are the teenage years when the flow of chatter becomes a series of grunts and when the actions of your children seem designed to be continually testing the boundaries. There is still a child in an adult's body: the need for love, possibly in a more subtle way, is as strong as ever. Keeping up the love but varying the approach with teenagers is perhaps the best possible in-service training anyone can have, enabling them to cope with difficult situations at work just as readily as at home!

As children move into their twenties, the joy of parenthood gets stronger and not less. The sense of responsibility as a parent is just as evident; you worry abut your children just as much when they are older. Your children can become your best counsellors and advisers because they know you so well. There may be periods of separation as independence is established, but then the emotional interdependence can become ever stronger and more joyful.

Whatever the age of the children, a key question is how to keep the dynamic of the relationships:

- *How can the family enjoy repeatedly what has been special to them as a family? (Every holiday we always play mock bridge because we've always enjoyed it as a family and it brings back*

---

memories of playing the game with three grandparents.)

- *What can you do with the family that is different?*
- *How can you create special family times either on holiday or at weekends, even after the children have left home?*

But our family is different

Talk of the 'nuclear family' can produce sadness or anger. Why have we not been able to have children? Why did the relationship with my partner break up? Why have I never found somebody who I want to live with over an extended period? Why is my sexuality such that I do not fit into a 'normal' pattern?

Maybe some of the key questions are:

- *What are the frustrations of my current situation? Can I define them very clearly?*
- *To what extent are these things givens that cannot be changed? Are there ways in which I can turn them into a positive foundation for the future?*
- *What can I change and what do I want to change?*
- *How do I develop the courage to make the changes that I want to make?*
- *How do I develop the courage to enjoy my different and therefore special family circumstances?*
- *How can I most enjoy my singleness and use it for good?*

Seeing the positive in these situations is never easy, but not being able to have children can give you the freedom to pursue your career and to travel more. Living alone can give you the time to pursue a wider range of cultural interests. Having your own separate base can give you time that is your own, with nobody else fighting their way into it.

Singleness can be a blessing and a joy. It provides maximum flexibility. There is no reason why it should be regarded as second best. It is the choice of many who enjoy their own company. For others, it is not their preferred option but can provide a richness of new friends and experiences.

Supporting our wider family

How can we best support those within our wider family? In our busy lives, months can pass with limited contact with them. In one sense this doesn't matter. Yet periodic contact with our wider family reinforces the strength of our heritage and the distinctive nature of what we bring as individuals to our families and communities.

Do we:

- *celebrate our nieces and nephews enough?*
- *find enough time to be available to our godchildren?*
- *create the opportunities for family gatherings?*
- *support family members who are struggling in practical ways?*

Jesus told the story of the shepherd who discovered that one of his sheep was missing. He went out and searched for the lost sheep until it was found and brought it back into the fold. Sometimes bringing back the lost sheep is part of our parental responsibility.

Treasuring our parents

Our parents are the mum and dad who brought us up, the

grandparents who enjoy the grandchildren, the elderly people who struggle with physical and possibly mental health issues. Eventually they become memories as we become the senior members of the family.

How we treasure our parents and the memories that we have of them is so important to our well-being as we move on ourselves into other spheres:

- *In what physical ways do we treasure the memories of our parents? What gifts from them have centre stage?*
- *Do we sometimes visit the places that were dear to us and our parents?*
- *Do we keep talking about special times with our parents?*
- *How are we continuing their heritage in the way we make our choices?*

Moving on to new beginnings

Five practical ways of thinking about your family:

- *Do you fully understand the impact that your family background has had on you?*
- *Are you making conscious, deliberate decisions about your family's future?*
- *Are you nurturing the bonds of love with your family enough?*
- *Do you understand the causes of guilt or anger in yourself?*
- *Can you move on effectively with family being a source of mutual support?*

Jennie's story

Jennie's father had died when she was young and the need to fulfil his expectations had spurred her on to a successful career. Her husband was hugely ambitious for Jennie and, after losing his job, he pinned a lot of expectations on his wife. She had a young daughter and wanted to spend more time with her, yet she was the breadwinner and needed to move on in her career. She recognised that now was a transition point in her life.

Jennie was beginning to stand back and make conscious decisions for herself rather than being pushed on someone else's treadmill. She was standing back from the expectations of her father and her husband. It was tough, but gradually she was beginning to get her priorities into shape. Her love for her late father and for her spouse was as strong as ever, but she also needed to express her love for her child in a way that was personal to her and her own conscious choice. The results were radical decisions about her career and a binding together of her family.

> *" I do not know who my grandfather was: I am much more concerned to know what his grandson will be. "*
>
> Abraham Lincoln

Chapter 6

FRIENDS

*" A friend is a person with whom I may be sincere.
Before him I may think aloud. "*

Ralph Waldo Emerson

*" A faithful friend is a sturdy shelter: they who find
one have found a treasure. "*

Ecclesiasticus

Where do friends fit into our life's journey? Are our friends a
major source of encouragement or embarrassment? Do we
nurture our friends enough or sometimes do we rather take
them for granted? Are we both enjoying the best of friendships and cultivating new friendships? Perhaps our friends are
our biggest source of encouragement on our life's journey.
Nurturing these friendships is nearly always worth the
investment.

Enjoying our companions on the way

A fridge magnet has printed on it, 'You are a friend for life: you
know too much about me.' I treasure my friends from my teenage
years when I was part of a lively youth group in Bridlington.
Members of the group have ended up in a variety of different
places, including teaching physics on the Isle of Wight, making
videos in Wiltshire, running the administration of a university

department in Leeds, working in a library in Beverley and doing auditing in Bridlington. That tight bond of friendship at the age of 17 or 18 lives on in a special way even though our personal circumstances are all very different. The friendship is kept alive by occasional meetings and telephone calls, but when we meet there is a richness of history and intimacy which allows the friendship to continue where it left off.

From university days I have a number of friends with whom there is an instant re-connect. These are people with whom I can think aloud: so often I know what I think when I hear myself say it. The openness with these friends helps stretch my thinking into new areas.

Think of the friends you have had the longest:

- *When did you first meet?*
- *What was it that produced an intimacy of friendship?*
- *How has that friendship continued to grow?*
- *What does that friendship continue to mean to you?*
- *How will it continue to grow further?*

Can you identify friends from each stage in your life? For me, there are the families we spent time with when our children were very small, three former work colleagues with whom I have a strong ongoing bond of friendship, and some special friends from our time living in Durham.

Wonderful things can emerge from friendships, such as:

- *an openness to share weaknesses as well as joys;*
- *a willingness to be challenged by friends while showing vulnerability;*

- *an acceptance that when I am feeling down I need not hide myself away from these friendships.*

If you reflect on the friendships that are most important to you, what would you define as the most essential ingredients? Are they:

- *a common experience?*
- *a shared sense of humour?*
- *the ability to tackle issues or discussions in a similar way?*
- *the nature of the trust between you?*
- *the intimacy of sharing?*

Rekindling friendships

Sometimes friendships begin to erode as life gets too busy. A conscious effort is needed to bring them back into a new focus. Sometimes it must be right to let friendships slip away: the common purpose or the need has gone. But that is not necessarily the end of the friendship. There are few things more joyful than picking up an old friendship many years on, when you are back with the same level of rapport as you had in earlier days.

Sometimes friendships do need rekindling. The telephone or the e-mail provide such a good opportunity to make the first step back in friendship. We need to prioritise our time: whenever I am tempted to watch a television programme, I say to myself I must make a phone call and talk to a real person. Whereas the phone can be such a blessing, the square screen can be such a curse in destroying the time for friendship.

One person I know has a very explicit list of the friends who are most important to her. She and her husband make every effort to see these friends individually at least once every six months. It is a very tight discipline which she regards as crucial to the success of these friendships.

Making new friends

When our children were teenagers they would often bring friends home. I relished this opportunity to talk to teenagers and university students: sometimes my children had to drag these people away. Was I interrogating their friends? No, I was just enjoying them so much.

Enjoying new people is also part of my work. I recently spent 24 hours with all the senior staff of a national organisation. As a facilitator I was meeting them in large and small groups. It was as if I had been given 150 new friends. It was for a short period but it was such a pleasure to talk with a number of them about specific things of interest to them.

We can regard the instant friendship as superficial and trivial. But the biggest gift an individual can possess is to be able to create a quick bond of friendship. Getting on somebody's wavelength and finding a common interest is a gift. My coaching work is based around trying to create a professional friendship very quickly whereby there can be openness and respect which allow a depth of mutual understanding.

How do you assess your ability to make new friendships? How easy do you find it to differentiate between professional friendships for a particular purpose, be it at work or in the community, and deeper friendships? The friendships at the school gate, in the gym, at the church or mosque or in the workplace are just as important for our well-being, even though they may be based on one aspect of our life. These brief exchanges are valuable because they raise our spirits and can lead to deeper friendships. They are part of the 'weft and warp' of community life.

Fleeting friendships can also surprise you by pointing you towards the future, or giving you a glimpse of a possible change of life. When I attended a weekend conference at a college in Cambridge in 2001, I talked to David Westcott, an executive coach, over tea. We had not met before but he shared with me his joys about his work. That conversation lit a flicker of light in me which eventually led to a radical career change, with the result that today I too am an executive coach. My pleasure in being a coach is primarily the pleasure of being a professional friend.

How might you develop deeper friendships with different people? Might it be with:

- *colleagues at work?*
- *parents of your children's friends?*
- *fellow members of community, sports or religious groups?*
- *those you come across who are lonely and need friendship?*

Mentoring one another

The most powerful friendships are two-way, where there is a strong sense of encouragement and challenge between one person and another. I often used to walk over Westminster Bridge with a colleague at the end of the day. We would talk about what had gone well and what had gone less well. When we felt we had failed we talked about it, and when we felt things had gone well we shared the joy. The conversations put things into perspective. Nothing could be more important in terms of bringing sanity to often demanding and irrational situations.

Mentoring is about bringing a wider perspective and helping somebody work through particular issues. It is about bringing wise counsel and drawing on personal experience. A senior member of the Crown Prosecution Service, in her advice to up-and-coming young people, talks of 'getting a mentor or three'. Building a network of mentors can provide us with great support that enables us to enrich others when we mentor them.

Bring generosity into friendship

Generosity is a two-way process. Bringing generosity into friendship may be about hospitality and graciousness. More than likely, it will be about time. Sometimes the time has to be elastic, but on other occasions it is focused, undivided attention for two or three minutes that can produce an uplift. It is the quality and not the quantity of time that makes the difference so often. Generosity is about seeing the best side of people and giving them the benefit of the doubt. It is about banishing criticism and not making judgements about why somebody has made the decisions they have. It is about providing a 'loaf of bread' willingly to the neighbour who asks for it.

The generosity of friendship is also about receiving generosity. Sometimes it is harder to receive than to give. Jeanette lost her husband a year ago. She was shocked but reopened old friendships and nurtured the ones that had been especially important to her. She let people be generous to her. Gradually her confidence came back: she moved house. She was open to the generosity of others and was renewed through it.

Rebecca lost her husband a year earlier. She went into her shell and was not open to the generosity of those around her. Her friendships dwindled: she became lonely and resentful.

She had wanted to be independent and not accept the generosity of others. That was the cruellest thing she could have done to herself.

When friends let you down

Friendship is never a perfect pathway. We rub along with each other, sometimes upholding each other and sometimes bruising each other. We cause pain in our friendships, sometimes through insensitivity and sometimes because we know the other person will understand and we have just got to let go.

Sometimes there is deep pain. Sometimes we feel as if we have been deliberately wounded. We may have put a lot of work into a friendship and we feel ignored, dismissed and irrelevant. Sometimes all we can do is shrug our shoulders and say, 'Such is life.' Jesus put a lot of work into training 12 disciples and one of them betrayed him. If, out of every 12 people whom we help to grow, eventually just one disowns us, perhaps that is not a bad ratio.

Moving on to new beginnings

Five things to do to build strong friendships:

- *What time are you going to set aside to grow your oldest friendships?*
- *Can you build a mutual mentoring relationship with two or three people with whom you have a shared agenda?*
- *What new friendships are you going to build and grow?*
- *What friendships can you develop with people of different ages, cultures and circumstances?*
- *In what ways are you going to be more generous in friendships, both in giving and receiving?*

Sadeka's story

Sadeka had a demanding job. She always operated at a fast pace. Her energy was relentless. She brought the same intense activity into her family. Sometimes it all got too much. She was achieving a great deal and there was a lot of fulfilment, but she needed to vary the pace. She could not go on at this level of activity for ever.

She recognised that she needed to slow down or she would burn herself out. What helped most were her friends. There was a close group of nine friends who mattered to her more than anything else. These were her husband, her brother, her parents and five friends from school and university days. As she focused on thoroughly enjoying these friendships and renewing them, she brought a healthy balance back into her life. She was then equipped for the next phase of her very full life.

> *" I have lost friends, some by death ... others through the sheer inability to cross the street. "*
>
> Virginia Woolf

Chapter 7

FINANCE

> *" Money can't buy you friends, but it can buy you a better class of enemy. "*
>
> Spike Milligan

> *" If we command our wealth, we shall be rich and free: if our wealth commands us, we are poor indeed. "*
>
> Edmund Burke

Are your concerns about finance a noose around your neck? The necessity for finance cannot be ignored. We need economic systems that provide food and shelter. We take pride in our financial independence. We want to do the best for our children. And yet finance as an enabler can soon become finance as a despot. Can we stand back from our financial situation and accept that where our treasures are, there our heart will be also? This chapter explores how we can best steward our resources, the joys of giving, key priorities for expenditure and how we might use our resources differently.

Financial security
How important is financial security to us? When my father died, my mother decided that in order to look after a very unconfident child and an ill relative, she should not go back to work but should devote herself to her family. Money, as a

consequence, was tight, holidays were limited and expenditure on clothes was minimal. I grew up with a concern about financial security, and when I began working I always saved a significant proportion of my income. My concern was commendable but excessive. At times it has meant I have not been as adventurous as perhaps I should have been.

- *Where on the spectrum are you between a concern for financial security and a willingness to take some financial risks?*
- *What have been the key influences on you in how you view finance?*
- *How much of your attitude to finance comes from family circumstance?*
- *How important is it for you to have savings in the bank?*
- *What level of financial independence is crucial for you?*

How can we best steward our resources?

In the biblical parable of the talents, the servant who hides the talent in the ground is the one who falls out of favour with his master. The other two servants are commended for using their talents and doubling them. Using our financial resources wisely can give us huge freedom to be an influence for good in our communities. We built a family room at the back of our house which has been used extensively by the children. Now they are away at university, up to 30 members of a young people's group use the room every Tuesday evening. It is such a delight to see the room used in this way.

Ruth and David were left some money by Ruth's mother. They bought a small house near their flat by the sea. They generously let a wide range of people use the house for retreats and holidays. It provides such a place of tranquillity for so many. They are wisely stewarding their resources and making the house available to others as a place of relaxation, reflection and renewal.

Stewarding resources doesn't just mean doubling the value of the talents. It is about using them to generate happiness and optimism in others and to build firmer relationships with family and friends and those in need of encouragement.

The joy of giving

Tithing may seem a dated custom but is perhaps just as relevant now as it used to be. Giving away a regular portion of our income can provide the discipline that helps keep other priorities in proportion. Tax arrangements in most countries enable giving to be done in a very tax-efficient way. Supporting your favourite charitable causes is well worthwhile in itself, and it also provides an important morale booster: giving makes you feel better!

What are your current priorities for giving?

- *How much of your net income do you give away?*
- *What causes do you give to?*
- *What causes would you like to support in the future through financial aid?*
- *What proportion of your income would you like eventually to be giving away?*
- *What proportion of your ultimate inheritance do you wish to give away?*

Giving may seem an optional extra, but it can be a very important part of our fulfilment. Carefully selecting the charitable interest you want to support can be hugely fulfilling and can provide an immense source of pleasure. It can be a means of making a significant contribution back into our society.

Your key priorities for expenditure

If you take a detached look at the current way you allocate your resources:

- *what is the relative priority between your home, your family, yourself and giving away?*
- *what is the balance you would like to attain eventually?*
- *what areas of expenditure would you like to increase?*
- *what areas of expenditure would you like to reduce?*

A key question is: What type of expenditure helps to reinforce other aspects of your quality of life? Do we sometimes begrudge paying for certain things that might represent a better use of our resources?

- *Are we prepared to pay more for food that is better for us health-wise?*
- *Are we willing to pay for products which have been generated in an environmentally friendly way?*
- *If time together is very important to us as a family, how important is it to spend money on doing things together rather than individually?*
- *How important are holidays for family life or for our own renewal?*

This does not mean buying the most expensive holiday: it means creating the holiday environment that works best for a particular family. It might be that an inexpensive cottage in the country is the best sort of family holiday rather than an expensive hotel.

Are we caught by inverted snobbery? I sometimes take great pride in wearing old clothes. Our family car is now 17 years old. Our lawnmower is now worth more than this car. I take pride in the way we have used our resources carefully. But the car uses petrol inefficiently and is not very environmentally friendly. Perhaps we should have moved on long ago.

How might we use our resources more effectively?

In the story of the good Samaritan, the priest and then the scribe look at the wounded man and pass by on the other side. It is the Samaritan, the outcast, who carries the wounded man to the inn and provides the financial support necessary for a period of recovery. This is generosity which is expecting no return. He provides for the well-being of somebody who could have been just ignored. He not only takes the wounded man to an inn, but also provides the resources for him to be looked after. He 'goes the extra mile'.

Can you sit more lightly to your finances, in terms of:

- *opening up the use of your resources to other people?*
- *experimenting with living on a lower level of resource?*
- *giving a greater proportion of your resources away?*
- *stewarding your resources so as to provide benefit for others?*

The more we practise living on a lower level of resource, the more we will be able to accept a future where we might consciously decide to reduce our income in order to be able to spend more time doing the things that are most important to us.

As part of moving on, we need a very honest discussion with ourselves about how important finance is and how we can stretch our finances further. When our youngest son decided that the pocket-money we were giving him was inadequate, he decided to buy his clothes from charity shops. He became the best-dressed member of the family because of his willingness to be adaptable!

The phases of life

At different stages of our lives the financial pressures will change. Initially the mortgage may be huge, then there are the costs of bringing up children, followed by university fees. Then there is building up the pension fund. We seem to be on a treadmill, building up the necessary funds in the bank. Sometimes people may make a conscious decision to get off that treadmill and go for a job with a lower income stream but perhaps a greater sense of enjoyment and fulfilment. Such people may feel it is more important to spend time with the children than to earn another tranche of overtime.

In previous generations an individual's income was normally highest in the latter part of their career. In many cases the opposite is now true. The peak earning power may well be in the thirties (particularly for those in merchant banking) or possibly in the forties (especially for those in senior administrative roles). From 50 onwards a move away from full-time employment into part-time work can mean an increase in freedom and a significant reduction in income. Hence the importance of managing finances carefully, but also of preparing for the day when we will be living on a smaller level of resources. So our joys in life must revolve less around finance and more around the people we are with.

Having no money is a great source of worry. Having too much money can equally be a great burden.

Some key questions about finance might be:

- *How important is financial security to you?*
- *Is your attitude to finance entirely healthy?*
- *What level of financial security is important to you for the future?*
- *How much would it matter if your income were halved?*
- *How much more could you give away to charitable causes?*

Moving on to new beginnings
Five firm next steps might include:

- *Establish realistic goals for saving.*
- *Set up an emergency fund for when your financial position becomes more difficult.*
- *Consider other forms of investment in your family.*
- *Invest in your own training and development.*
- *Give away a measurable chunk of your income to a charity.*

Neil's story
Neil had worked with an international organisation in three continents. He loved his job and the challenges it brought him, and he loved working all over the world. Each move had been a major step up. His wife and family had come with him and had enjoyed the luxuries of international living. They had a comfortable lifestyle with a large property back home. They were set on a course to build up significant financial assets.

Everything looked as if it was going perfectly until Neil was made redundant. Suddenly finding himself without an income, he felt that everything was falling apart. A severance package was on offer. There was an opportunity for new beginnings, but one of his children was very ill. Somehow the big house and the large income did not seem to matter any more. What was most important was getting established again back home, building the family again and being rooted in a community. Gradually a completely different sort of career opened up back home, with a much greater emphasis on serving others. His child's illness made him realise what was important to him and stopped him wallowing in these difficult times. There was a quiet acceptance that 'the love of money' had been a source of unease. He developed much less ambitious aspirations about wealth. Now a strong sense of generosity was enabling his next steps to put his life back on an even keel. He had a secure, modest home, a close family and a new way of helping others through training work with adults. A new calmness pervaded Neil's relationships and priorities.

" There is no wealth but life. "

John Ruskin

Chapter 8
FUNDAMENTALS

> *" The fruit of the Spirit is love, joy, peace, patience, kindness, goodness, faithfulness, gentleness and self-control. "*
>
> Galatians 5

> *" You never know how much you really believe in anything until its truth and falsehood becomes a matter of life or death to you. "*
>
> C. S. Lewis

This is the tipping-point in this book, where we move from taking stock to looking forward. After looking at our attitude to friends, family and finance, we move into what is most important to us. Being as clear as possible about the fundamentals that matter most to you provides the clarity that enables you to move on.

What are your most fundamental beliefs about yourself and your world? What is more important to you than anything else? How do you want to be remembered? What are the values that you attach most importance to and which you are determined to live by? What do you want to see written on your tombstone?

What really matters

Henry was a board member of a major commercial organisation. His life had been devoted to his work where he had been hugely successful and was greatly respected for his openness and care for his staff. But something was missing. He had expected to be a lifelong bachelor but, in his late forties, he met the love of his life, left his job and had a wonderful 'gap year'. He was successful in getting another board-level post in a national organisation, but he now viewed the job in a rather different way. He was as determined as ever and continued to be an excellent manager and mentor, but he had now got a rather different set of priorities. His career was not the be all and end all. The objectivity of his judgement and contributions was all the stronger because there were other things that were even more important than his job. Doing an effective job as a senior leader mattered a great deal to him, but it sat alongside being with 'the love of his life' and sharing common values, experiences and delights with his partner.

What can we learn from Henry? Perhaps it is his openness to change, perhaps it is the way he was ready to be surprised, the way he was open to new ways of balancing his work and his family. Or perhaps it is the way he was still prepared to reassess what was fundamental to him and to build on that.

What have been the most important influences on you?

We looked at the importance of our family and cultural background in Chapter 5. It is clear that whether we like it or not, the most fundamental influences upon us are often our families and our culture.

It is not a matter of whether we love and respect our

parents; it is understanding as objectively as possible their influence upon us and how it has created the drivers and emotions within us. We cannot, and should not, blind ourselves to this reality.

In what ways have your family been a strong influence upon you in terms of:

- *your values?*
- *your behaviours?*
- *your beliefs?*
- *your aspirations?*
- *your fears?*

Being utterly clear about the influence of your family background provides a crucial starting-point. The second key influence is your culture. It may be a particular regional, ethnic, social or religious culture. Whatever the culture, it will have formed in you a set of values. My own background was a single-parent family, no siblings living at home, a small Yorkshire town, a Methodist heritage and limited financial resources within the family. The result was a rather serious, driven young man who was determined to be successful at university and in his career, and for whom walking by the sea, good friendships and faith were particularly important. I was a mix of characteristics that came largely from my cultural background.

As you reflect on your cultural background:

- *What were the biggest influences upon you?*
- *How are they manifested in your behaviour?*

- *How are these influences mutually reinforcing?*
- *What are the contradictions in you that come from your cultural background?*
- *How good have you been at reconciling those contradictions?*

How do you want to move on from your family and cultural background?

- *What is dear to you that you do not want to change?*
- *In what ways have you moved on from your family and cultural background?*
- *In what ways do you want to move on further from your background?*

What are the most important values to you?

Another way of looking at your fundamentals is to be very clear about what values are most important to you. Some people are clear about their values while other people will say they do not have particular values, but as soon as you begin to talk with them about what matters most to them, they begin to articulate a set of values.

Are your values (or what matters to you most) about:

- *how you engage with your family?*
- *how you engage with your friends?*
- *your participation in the community or culture in which you live?*
- *the impact you make at work?*
- *making a difference through the range of activities in which you are involved?*

A set of shared values we developed when I was a board member at the Department for Education and Skills (DfES) were:

- *We are determined to make a difference.*
- *We listen and value diversity.*
- *We are honest and open.*
- *We innovate and challenge.*
- *We learn and improve.*

Often the values we live by are in tension with each other. In the list of DfES values above there was sometimes a tension between being determined to make a difference, and listening and valuing diversity. The test is how well we can interrelate these different values together and balance the tensions.

It can be very helpful to note down:

- *the values that are most important to you;*
- *how you think those values are changing;*
- *how you want those values to change in the future.*

Where have you had the biggest impact?

As we reflect on where we have had our biggest impact, we become clearer about what is fundamentally important to us. As we reflect objectively on what our strengths are, we can be surer about the foundation on which we want to move forward.

Are our strengths about:

- *our drive and determination?*
- *our ability to show great depths of love?*

- *our sensitivity to the needs of others?*
- *our capacity for forgiveness?*
- *our ability to respond to difficult situations?*
- *the courage that can flow out of us in certain very demanding contexts?*

Whatever our strengths, it is crucial to celebrate them and regard them as a vital foundation for the future. The strengths are there to build on: it is not a matter of puffing up our strengths or hiding them. Putting our light under a bushel does nobody any good; neither does insensitively drawing attention to our own abilities.

How can you build on your strengths to help others towards their own success? This is where we can make a marked difference for the benefit of others:

- *If you are good at working in a team, how can you do more to help build the teams you are part of?*
- *If people open up with you, how can you use that openness to build up their confidence?*
- *If you can see needs in individual people, how can you respond to that in a way which respects their boundaries and yet takes them to new levels of understanding?*
- *If you are good at getting projects done, how can you use that strength for the good of your community or to help your colleagues?*

Where do personal beliefs fit in?
Our lives are a sequence of journeys. There is the journey from childhood through the teenage years to adulthood and to

eventual retirement. There is also the journey of faith and belief: as a child we adopt the perspective of our parents and culture, whether it be one of faith or no faith. In our teenage years we are likely to rebel to some degree against whatever has been our background.

Asking fundamental questions about ourselves and our future includes questions about faith and belief just as much as questions about our background, our values, our aspirations and ambitions. Do not pass over this subject as irrelevant and a waste of time. At moments of 'finding your future', being clear to yourself about where faith and belief fit in provides a key foundation, whatever you decide. It is a crucial part of your reaching a conclusion about what is your purpose in life.

Just as you spend time developing physical fitness, or emotional awareness of both yourself and those with whom you live and work, religious awareness is a perfectly valid way of developing your own humanity. It may be through understanding more of the richness of different faith traditions, talking issues through with friends or through being solitary and reflecting quietly about your place within the universe. There might just be a small still voice of calm, courage or compassion that flows into you as you explore your awareness of faith and belief.

Where does your energy come from?

Another fundamental is to establish what energises you and what doesn't. If there is some activity that gives you energy, how can you do more of it? It may be running, swimming, French polishing, or leading a study group at church. You enjoy it and you feel it is particularly worthwhile. If it gives you energy that flows into other parts of your life, then it is a precious thing that you should develop.

Being clear about our fundamentals is about fully understanding our background, values, beliefs and, crucially, where our energy comes from. When I help prepare people for interview, I ask them what makes them passionate about the job, what would excite them if they were in that particular role. If there is no passion and no excitement, they will neither do the job well nor communicate effectively in an interview.

As you move forward:

- *What are your greatest strengths?*
- *What are you passionate about?*
- *What will excite you most over the next few years?*
- *What will give you the greatest sense of fulfilment?*

Measuring yourself against your fundamentals

Part of looking forward is about clarity about your background, values, beliefs and sources of energy: it is also being clear how you want to assess your own progress. How do you want to measure the extent to which you are living your fundamentals? This is not about creating a rod to beat yourself up with, but it is about clarity in understanding your own progress on your life's journey.

Maybe you should write down each year:

- *What are the fundamentals that have been most important to me?*
- *In what areas have I built on those fundamentals?*
- *What has enabled me to make the most progress?*

- *What has held me back?*
- *What are my next steps?*

Moving on to new beginnings

Five key issues to reflect on concerning what is fundamental to you as you move into your future:

- *How crucial have your family and culture been? How much of this heritage do you want to embed or change?*
- *Which are your most important values that you want to build on?*
- *What are your core beliefs that are most important to you?*
- *Where does your energy come from and how can you draw more on that source of energy?*
- *In ten years' time, how do you want to be remembered?*

George's story

George had flowed easily into university and then into his career. He had gifts of analysis, clarity of thinking and the ability to build rapport with a wide range of people. He made people feel at ease who then easily told him of their priorities and concerns. He built networks effectively. His work and the family from which he came were his life.

He was posted to work in Asia and met a very special person. In his friendship with this person a whole new dimension to his life became clear. He enjoyed the friendship and engagement with her family. But what was most important to him: his life back in his home country, his career, or his new friendship? He was balancing enjoying his heritage, living out independent values, developing a belief in what was most important, and wrestling with where his energy most effectively came from. Not the easiest of choices. Working through what is most fundamental to us is never straightforward, but he was making progress and gradually working out what was most important for him.

> *" Only love enables humanity to grow, because love engenders life, and it is the only form of energy that lasts for ever. "*
>
> Michel Quoist

LOOKING FORWARD

Looking forward is where the hard work begins. It is where boldness in our thinking and action becomes important. There may be very different strands in looking forward, such as:

- the importance of *forgiveness*, especially of ourselves;
- following our *fascinations*;
- being clear about the degree of *freedom* we have and how we want to use it;
- the use of *fasting* and self-denial as an aid.

Sometimes it is only when forgiveness takes root that we can begin to look forward with untarnished sight. Allowing ourselves to follow our fascinations can take us out of ourselves into a new perspective. Realism about the degree of freedom we do or do not have is essential. Fasting or self-denial may be one element of preparing for our next steps.

You will move on from this section with a clearer head and less clutter. You will be clearer on what are your priorities for the future. Your heart and head are more likely to be speaking the same language.

Chapter 9
FORGIVENESS

" Twas grief enough to think mankind
All hallow, servile, insincere
But worse to trust to my own mind
And find the same corruption there. "

Emily Brontë

" Forgiveness is the key that unlocks the door of resentment and the handcuffs of hate. It is a power that breaks the chains of bitterness and the shackles of selfishness. "

Corrie ten Boom

Is forgiveness something other people do? Is forgiveness quite difficult for us to do in a meaningful way? We can easily say 'sorry' when something small goes wrong. But when there is a major problem and we have been badly hurt, forgiveness does not come that easily. And forgiving ourselves – well, that is in a completely different league altogether and can be much, much tougher. But as we forgive, finding our future will become that much easier.

Facing harsh realities
Ronan was attending a church service in South Africa. He had arrived late and was not sitting with his son or wife. Militant

soldiers burst open the door, shots were fired, and he threw himself under the pew. When the shooting ended he searched for his family and discovered that his son was dead. He embraced his dead son and immediately said he forgave the gunman.

For months he wrestled with his grief and went into deep depression, for he had forgiven in words but it took time to work through his pain. He needed to talk about his anger. The gunmen were identified and said they regretted their action, which helped a little, as it was a milestone in the healing process. Eventually Ronan moved out of the depression as life moved on and he was fully able to embrace the forgiveness which was very important to him. Forgiveness was now in his heart as well as his words.

The story illustrates that there may be a time-lag between saying you forgive and the forgiveness becoming fully embedded. The first act is the conscious decision to forgive, but it may be some time before your emotions have caught up. True forgiveness often only happens after some time has passed and a grief process has been worked through.

We have no difficulty in forgiving the toddler in a tantrum, the five-year-old who will not eat his tea, the 11-year-old who comes home coated in mud or the 13-year-old who crashes her bike. It becomes more difficult, maybe, when it is the 16-year-old who gets drunk, the 17-year-old who has taken some drugs or the 18-year-old who just refuses to work for their exams.

A key starting-point is reflection on:

- *How easily do we forgive?*

- *What helps us to forgive?*
- *How readily is forgiveness embedded?*
- *Is resentment a risk for us?*

How good are we at forgiveness?

Forgiveness is not about 'anything goes'. Forgiveness sits alongside the values that are most important to us.

What are the examples of forgiveness by you that you particularly remember? Was it:

- *one of the children in your life testing the boundaries?*
- *a family member who was not there when you needed them?*
- *a neighbour who let you down?*
- *a colleague who misrepresented you?*

What was it that best enabled you to forgive that person? Was it:

- *the strength of the long-term friendship?*
- *your recognition of the stress they were under?*
- *their apology?*

In what ways did your being able to forgive help? Did it:

- *reinforce the strength of the friendship?*
- *enable there to be a new phase in the relationship?*
- *enable you to move on and not feel resentment?*

When did you find it most difficult to forgive?

- *When you personally were hurt?*
- *When a close friend or family member was wronged?*
- *When you were manipulated?*

Forgiveness is not a sign of weakness: it is an expression of strength. Genuine forgiveness can make us vulnerable, as the recipient may take advantage of that forgiveness. But without forgiveness the relationship cannot move on. Forgiveness is a serious, difficult business. In the words of C. S. Lewis, 'Everyone says forgiveness is a lovely idea, until they have something to forgive.'

How often should we forgive? Is it really seven times seventy times? Forgiveness does not mean ignoring the root of a problem. It does not mean hiding from the realities of a difficult situation. When someone has been wronged, fairness and justice sit alongside forgiveness. Forgiveness also involves a recognition of a will to change.

Sometimes our forgiveness may be reasonably straight-forward: for example, when one of the children in your life keeps letting themselves down, or when a colleague has made a mistake and is determined to learn from it. Forgiveness may not be as easy when a colleague manipulates what you say in a damaging way or a friend abuses your trust.

It might be helpful to reflect on:

- *How easily does forgiveness come to you?*
- *When do you find it most difficult to forgive?*
- *What helps you forgive?*
- *What helps you move on and put the issue behind you?*

Finding our future will often involve coming to terms with situations or relationships where there is resentment, and sometimes there will be an oscillation between resentment and forgiveness. As an example, Geoffrey thought long and hard about whether he should move on from his current employer. His boss wanted him to stay in order to help ensure an effective transition into a new phase of the organisation. But once the reorganisation was complete, his boss wanted Geoffrey to move on and forced him to leave. The fact that the financial exit arrangements were good helped up to a point.

At his lowest moments, Geoffrey felt that his loyalty had been abused. At his best moments he was grateful for the push into a new sphere which he greatly enjoyed. Geoffrey needed to forgive his boss for what he felt had been harsh treatment. Intellectually he could do this, but emotionally there were the occasional shafts of resentment about the way he had been treated. What was so crucial for Geoffrey were two or three close friendships where he could just occasionally sound off about his resentment. Gradually there was genuine healing.

It was vital for Geoffrey to talk through his resentment and understand it. Denying the existence of the resentment would not have helped, neither would have confronting his former boss with the resentment. He needed to accept that he would oscillate between forgiveness and resentment before there would be genuine forgiveness.

Geoffrey had to reach the point of wanting to move on from resentment. Sometimes it can be very comfortable to wallow in, and even enjoy resentment. Moving on from this ambivalence often needs the combination of an external jolt and the consistent warm embrace of those we love.

Forgiveness as a cathartic next step

Moving on so often depends on a very explicit decision to forgive those who cause resentment in us. It isn't necessarily that they have done anything wrong. It is just that they have taken decisions with a different set of objectives or values and we have become the 'fall guy'. Sometimes only a very explicit act enables us to move on.

That may involve:

- *a very honest conversation with the person concerned;*
- *articulating the anger very fully with a close friend;*
- *a very deliberate financial gift to a charity which marks the transition;*
- *a special celebration with those close to you, with that sense of joy overshadowing the resentment.*

It may well not be a matter of completely expunging the resentment: it may be reducing it gradually until it disappears into insignificance. Mother Teresa once wrote, 'It is by forgiving that one is forgiven.'

When have you been forgiven?

It is very helpful to look at what it feels like to be forgiven. Sometimes we can only move on when we have explicitly sought forgiveness. In an earlier chapter I told the story of encouraging my seven-year-old daughter to go on a round-about which began to travel vertically rather than just horizontally. I was as close to panic as I have ever been. As she grew older I needed a sense of forgiveness from my daughter because I had unwittingly put her in a potentially dangerous situation. That explicit sense of forgiveness was crucial to minimise my occasional nightmares about that evening in Sunderland. How does it feel to be forgiven? Do you sense that combination of relief and release?

Once, in the midst of difficult financial negotiations, a key figure had been missed. I had overall responsibility and wanted to protect the two people who had been doing the detailed figure-work. The Minister of the day showed remarkable equanimity and expressly said that he understood what had happened and was in no way going to bear a grudge. That assurance was so important both for me and the team.

It might be helpful to reflect on:

- *When have you felt forgiven?*
- *What effect did reassuring words have on you?*
- *Were you able to mirror in your behaviour that experience of forgiveness?*

Forgiving yourself: the most difficult form of forgiveness

If forgiving others is sometimes tough, forgiving ourselves is in another league altogether.

We continue to beat ourselves up about:

- *Why did I not spend more time with my ageing parents?*
- *Why did I have to spend so much time at work?*
- *Why did I not recognise the difficulties my children were facing?*
- *Why did I not understand the controversy I was walking into?*
- *Why did I not look after myself better and avoid the current health problem?*
- *Why did I have to drive so fast?*

Bringing to the surface the 'why' questions is important. We have to be honest with ourselves, but continually beating ourselves up is no solution.

Sometimes we need to be very honest about why we took certain decisions:

- *We worked hard because we wanted to provide a relaxing home for our family.*
- *We worked the extra hours in order to have the enjoyable family holidays.*
- *We were very single-minded on a particular project in order to ensure its success.*

It was not that we were being selfish or irresponsible; we took certain steps because we cared. It might be that, in retrospect, we think we misplaced our energies. I thought my daughter would enjoy the roundabout ride in Sunderland: I was as shocked as she was when it began travelling vertically and not just horizontally. Telling myself that I acted with the best of intentions helps me forgive myself for what was a rather foolish thing to do.

Sometimes the explanation we give ourselves is not very good. We cannot just fall back on, 'Well, we did it for the best of motives.' Sometimes we have put ourselves in positions which almost inevitably have led to problems. It might be the job that was almost undoable, or the relationship that was almost bound to fail, or the risk that had everything stacked against it. Objectively, it was a foolish act to embark on this step. Forgiving ourselves for what we accept as foolishness is such an important cathartic act. Only then can the process of healing really begin.

Sometimes our intentions have not been so honourable. We may have been vain, greedy or selfish. At the time we thought we were being just a touch foolhardy, but in retrospect we cannot deny that our motives do not stand up to scrutiny. Forgiving ourselves in this situation often only comes after a period of painful remorse. But even in these situations there can be a moving on.

Where does confession fit in?

All the major religious traditions have a focus on confession. Genuine confession helps us move on, but confession does not put a wrong right. The young offender showing remorse may see their sentence reduced but the crime has still been committed. Genuine confession certainly helps us move on: sometimes that confession can be to the individual concerned, or to an independent third party, or a shared confession in a wider faith community. Genuine confession cannot be entered into lightly but can be a very powerful source of renewal, provided there is a genuine sense of moving on.

Moving on to new beginnings

Five crucial steps about forgiveness:

- *Be clear whether you really want to forgive somebody and move on from enjoying the resentment.*
- *Be ready to explicitly show forgiveness.*
- *Take action to work resentment gradually out of your system.*
- *Decide on what steps you are going to take to forgive yourself.*
- *Be explicit in defining how important forgiveness is as part of finding your future.*

Norman's story

Norman worked hard at his job and enjoyed the analytic work, but he didn't find it that easy to relate to his boss. Norman had a broad smile and an apparently equitable temperament, but he did not always get his priorities right in the way he spent his time. He got bogged down in detail, with the distance widening between himself and his boss.

Gradually he became more and more resentful inside. He became cross with himself and his boss and most of the rest of the world. He found it really hard to be decisive in the way he used his time. A vicious circle was creating indecisiveness and resentment. He had to want to prioritise effectively: he had to begin to make some progress in building a better relationship with his boss. The only way he was going to move on was through a combination of forgiving himself and forgiving his boss. Only then was there going to be a clarity of purpose unblinkered by his emotions. But could he reach that point?

" Forgiveness is not an occasional art, it is a permanent attitude. "

Martin Luther

Chapter 10

FASCINATIONS

" I will lift up mine eyes unto the hills, from whence cometh my help. "

Psalm 121

" I can only look for something that I have, to some degree, already found. "

Henri Nouwen

What are your fascinations? Where does your curiosity take you? When you dream dreams, what do you see and experience? When you have followed your fascinations, has it taken you down new avenues? Have daydreams led you to new horizons? Where might following your fascinations take you in the future?

What are your fascinations?

Today we are going to St James's Palace in London with two of our children, where they will receive their Duke of Edinburgh Gold Awards. We will be the proud parents of two youngsters who followed their fascinations and participated in a scheme which encourages young people to follow up different interests and reach a level of expertise in them. The required five-day hike through the Welsh mountains was more a test of determination than an opportunity to dream dreams – other

---

than dreams of a decent bed and home cooking at the end of the walk.

The scheme encouraged them to try different things. To our complete surprise, our daughter decided to do rock climbing. We responded with our mouths open, 'Well, of course.' Our son followed various sporting interests which eventually led to his captaining the UK Youth Ultimate Frisbee Team in the World Championships in Finland. As they followed their fascinations, we stood back and watched, sometimes in trepidation and at other times as glowing parents!

Following fascinations is not an indulgence. It is part of the way we grow and test our own boundaries. Watching the professional doing their job well often creates a fascination to follow that particular route, be it as a footballer, a teacher or a police officer.

Look back to when you were a teenager:

- *What were the fascinations that caught your imagination?*
- *Which of those fascinations did you follow up?*
- *Which of them led down a blind alley?*
- *Which fascinations helped you grow in understanding or knowledge?*
- *What did you learn from following those fascinations?*

Following fascinations is about developing the gift of curiosity. As a teenager:

- *What were your sources of curiosity?*
- *Who helped you stretch your willingness to be curious?*
- *Was following your curiosity a source of joy or pain?*

Following fascinations does not always lead to the promised land. We have got to be honest about what we tried to do and failed at. Sometimes following our fascinations might have led down pathways which we now regard as indulgences, from an excessive love of football to the taking of soft drugs. However futile the fascination, there will always have been learning about ourselves and about what we now regard as most important.

Fascinations that are waiting to be released

As you look back to your teenage years or your twenties, are there fascinations that you wish you had followed? Such as:

- *the skill you did not develop;*
- *the authors you would have learned from;*
- *the places you wanted to discover;*
- *the expeditions you would have enjoyed.*

It is well worth:

- *listing these fascinations;*
- *reflecting on which of them are still important to you and why;*
- *considering whether there are some that you would like to take further forward.*

Barry had had a successful career and had held posts with lots of responsibility. He was now looking at standing back a little and moving to working three days a week. He was unsure whether he really wanted extra time on his hands. He wanted to give his life some structure. Cycling had long been a fascination. He admired his friends who cycled and wanted to emulate them. The result was that he bought a new bike and he and his wife got enormous pleasure from going for long cycle rides. This not only fulfilled a lifelong fascination but also kept him fit! Following his interest in cycling was not indulgence but was an important part of building his future.

Another of Barry's dreams had been to learn how to play the trumpet. There was initial enthusiasm, but then taking the trumpet lessons went on the back burner. He would do it in the autumn, he promised himself. He asked his friends to hold him to account on this. He had been very successful as a senior manager, but he was not sure that developing a skill as a brass player would come easily. He was a little reluctant to embark on something where he might feel a bit humiliated. For Barry, following the fascination of cycling had opened new interests and pleasures for him. But how far would a fear of failure inhibit him from learning the trumpet? Some fascinations are easier to follow than others, some involve more fear than others. But only by exploring them can we find out which ones are going to 'take off'.

Dream dreams

At one stage my eldest son kept saying to me, 'Pretend you are 21 again.' He challenged me to dream dreams, and those dreams had to be rooted in who I was and who I really wanted to be. The dreams could not be mere fantasies: it was all about stretching my thinking. I followed a couple of fascinations about a possible second career. Going down one path, the fascination rapidly began to disappear. Going down another path, I was clearly the wrong person at the wrong place at the wrong time: I had to face up to reality.

So my son challenged me again: 'Pretend you are 21 again. What do you really enjoy doing?' My response was, 'Talking to people one-to-one and encouraging them.' So with his support, I ended up working as an executive coach. I am indebted to my son for pushing me to follow that fascination and to dream dreams about moving into a completely different world.

Following fascinations can require a huge amount of courage. James was a manager who had done pretty well in his career. He had started work when he was aged 18 and had moved through a variety of interesting jobs. He dreamed of being a primary school teacher. But there was the mortgage, there were the pension rights that he had built up, there was the respect in which he was held in his current world. It would be a pretty brave step to do a career switch in his mid forties. The idea came and went and came back a bit: maybe one day, but not now.

There must always be a reality test. Our responsibilities to our families are important. We have to choose which fascinations to follow. Some may have to remain as dreams for now. Others can be the bedrock for our next steps.

It is worth being utterly objective:

- *In your work situation, how content are you?*
- *Does following your fascinations mean stretching the boundaries in terms of what you do in your current role?*
- *Does following your fascinations mean exploring other avenues?*
- *Are you clear about which two or three other avenues you might want to explore?*

What are the boundaries to following your fascinations?

- *How restrictive are your financial commitments?*
- *What is the perspective of your partner and those nearest to you?*
- *What would be the effect on the children in your life?*
- *Would following your fascinations be detrimental or beneficial to your health?*
- *Would taking forward your fascinations give you energy or sap your energy?*

At one level, following your fascinations may mean switching the type of work you do. We live in an age where there is a wealth of training and development opportunities and an acceptance that specific jobs are not for life. The flipside of the uncertainties of employment in the twenty-first century is the recognition that changing one's career in mid life is not necessarily an expressions of madness!

Following fascinations may be about a change of career or it may be about following up a whole range of different interests. When I worked in the North-East of England for a couple of years, my wife Frances followed up her fascination with theology by doing a master's degree at Durham University which eventually led to a doctorate, teaching at graduate level and the publication of a book. It was unclear at first where her fascination was going to lead, but it led down a rich pathway.

The mustard seed is a very tiny object. You might well need your glasses on to see it. But from this tiny seed grows a substantial shrub. A small fascination can grow into a very productive outcome.

Learning from fascinations

Last Christmas Frances and I spoke about the places that

fascinated us, and we highlighted Iceland and Boston. With the children now at university, we decided to follow those fascinations. We were enthralled by the geysers and lakes in Iceland, and we walked the Freedom Trail in Boston. We had found cheap flights and stayed at basic hotels. We decided that now was the time to follow the fascinations while we were still fit enough to enjoy them. Being bold in following our fascinations helped us to move on and get used to the reality that all three of our children had now left home.

The Christian Church began from 12 people who were fascinated by what Jesus, their leader, was saying. They did not understand his words all the time. It took three years for their curiosity to grow into the dream of sharing the wisdom of this itinerant teacher. After Jesus had left them their fascination with his life and work led to the dream of a different sort of community.

Where might your fascinations take you?

It is important to take the time to listen to yourself and ask yourself serious questions about your fascinations:

- *Are there burning fascinations you have always wanted to pursue?*
- *Is there a glimmer of an interest that you have always been a little curious about?*
- *What doors might you want to push ajar to see if they might open?*
- *Who are your companions on the way?*

Moving on to new beginnings

Five practical next steps:

- *Be explicit about your learning through following particular fascinations.*
- *Be clear about which fascinations either burn in your heart or are a bright glimmer.*
- *Be objective about the realism of these fascinations.*
- *Reflect on where you want your curiosity to take you.*
- *Share with friends which fascinations you are now going to follow up.*

Margot's story

Margot had been a successful teacher and was a capable organiser. When her three children were at school she became a very efficient receptionist at a doctor's surgery, but this wasn't fulfilling her and there was a growing restlessness. After going back into teaching for a while, she decided it wasn't for her. Working as the administrator at her local church only fulfilled part of her potential. There was a strong sense of service, with a growing sense of wanting to contribute in a local church as part of the ordained leadership. Was she called to this vocation? Initially she was told 'No' after attending a national assessment.

She never gave up on following her dream and her sense of calling. Her friends kept supporting and encouraging her. After the initial No, a couple of years later there was a resounding Yes. Seeing her lead the funeral of a dear friend, with 400 people in the congregation, was such a powerful indicator that she was now in the right role. Following her dream had led her on a pathway to contributing in a way that meant a great deal to people wrapped in sadness. She brought hope and encouragement in the depths of grief. We were so glad that she had determinedly followed her dream.

" Do not walk through time without leaving worthy evidence of your passage. "

Pope John XXII

Chapter 11

FREEDOM

" People hardly ever make use of the freedom they have, for example the freedom of thought; instead they demand freedom of speech as a compensation. *"*

Søren Kierkegaard

" Where we are free to act, we are also free not to act, and where we are able to say no, we are able to say yes. *"*

Aristotle

How much freedom do we really want? We enjoy living in a 'free' country. We take pride in a democracy that enables us to make choices. But do we allow ourselves to be boxed in and limit our own freedom, denying ourselves the freshness that comes from testing the boundaries? The best of freedom is not anarchy but a structured way of looking at each issue, to see what are the constraints and what are the opportunities.

How much freedom do we want?

I chatted with a taxi driver called John recently as he drove me from Edinburgh Airport into the centre of the city, and we talked about what freedom meant for him. He sort of enjoyed his work driving a taxi: the customers at the airport were always courteous and he would never want to cope with the drunkards in the city. He liked his routine: it was a job that brought him an income, but what sort of freedom did he really enjoy? It was going off to the golf course on a sunny afternoon for a quick nine holes before returning to the taxi rank at the Airport.

There was a wonderful ambivalence in John. He did not want too much freedom because the taxi driving gave him an income and a structure to his life. But there were those moments when 'playing hooky' and disappearing off to the golf course was just the tonic he needed.

Søren Kierkegaard's comment that 'People hardly ever make use of the freedom they have' is a salutary reminder. Perhaps we do put a lot of store on freedom of speech and rather less on freedom of thought. Are we very set in our ways?

When did we last:

- *change our minds on a major issue?*
- *try a radically different approach to solving a problem?*
- *decide we are going to move in a completely new direction?*
- *identify what our future choices are in an open-ended way?*

It may have been some time ago. This type of freedom is not something we embrace on a daily, monthly or even an annual basis. Freedom is unsettling and we get all too comfortable with our current arrangements, even if this comfort is not real contentment and satisfaction.

How deep rooted is our contentment with:

- *our work environment?*
- *our family and community lives?*

- *the way we spend our time?*
- *our approach to stretching our own thinking?*
- *the nature of our beliefs?*

How attractive is freedom to us?

How attractive do we find people for whom freedom is important? Do we identify with the skier racing down the mountain slope, the yachtsman pushed along by a firm breeze, the walker on a long-distance footpath or the child splashing excitedly in the paddling pool? Can you use pictures in your mind of these sorts of people as an inspiration?

Yes, but there are limits to freedom, we tell ourselves. What is our reaction to the teenager enjoying the freedom of taking drugs, the husband leaving his second partner and his fifth child, the politician jumping on the latest bandwagon, or the driver treating speed limits with reckless abandon?

We are horrified when freedoms are used irresponsibly and are soon ready to condemn, with testing the boundaries seen as a dangerous activity. Freedom does mean taking risks. Jean-Paul Sartre wrote, 'Once freedom has exploded in the soul of man, the gods have no more power over him.'

We see a balance between defining boundaries and taking unnecessary risk. We have 'freedoms from' and 'freedoms to'. Sometimes they are two sides of the same coin: the freedom from oppression and the freedom to make our own life choices Some uses of freedom we applaud; others we will want to condemn. Are we always rational and consistent?

It is worth reflecting on:

- *How consistent are we in our attitude to others' use of freedom?*

- *Do we condemn too easily rather than seek to understand?*
- *Have we got our balance between 'freedom from' and 'freedom to' right?*

Part of our role as parents is allowing children to experiment, often within boundaries that we choose. With young children, having clear boundaries provides freedom for them to grow within a framework. Knowing the boundaries is crucial for a young child, but compressing those boundaries too tightly can inhibit the growth of energy and independence. Letting go is a difficult task for parents with their teenage children, while trying to hold on to the heritage and values that they have tried to place at the centre of home life.

We might, as parents, take a 'responsible' view, allowing young people freedom and enabling them to learn, while at the same time taking a much more restrictive view about ourselves which limits our own freedom to grow and change. Sometimes we can be inconsistent for the best of reasons. Observing how we react to the way young people use their freedom can lead to important self-reflection. Do we react in a particular way because we feel our freedom is too curtailed? When we are critical of others, it is worth reflecting on why. Do we use the freedoms we have wisely and boldly?

What sort of freedom is most important to you? Is it the freedom:

- *to be creative in your work?*
- *to have flexibility in your work?*
- *to use your time differently?*
- *to build new friendships?*

- *to stretch your thinking and learning?*
- *to express yourself in different ways?*

What are our boundaries on freedom?

Freedom is not about acting irresponsibly. Clarity about our own values provides a vital framework. The importance of loving and cherishing our family is a key principle, but how often do we express that value in a rather predictable way? Consistency of love is vital, but some variety is crucial too. The mug of tea by the bedside each morning may be a simple, regular, kindly act: a welcome routine to start a busy day. But maybe that is balanced by the freedom to vary the menu in the evening, trying different dishes and spices.

As individuals, we may place great value on our chosen career. We may be committed to be a teacher or a nurse. But there is still the freedom to fulfil our vocation in a way that keeps stretching the boundaries and may sometimes mean using our skills in different ways. It may be a different group of children or a different school or hospital. The good teacher will always say that their lessons need to adapt to meet the circumstances of a particular group of children. If the teacher doesn't change and evolve their approach, they become stale.

How radical can we be in the place where we spend our working life, whether we're employed or working at home? Can we:

- *use our time differently, with more varied patterns?*
- *create just a modest amount of time to read?*
- *find some moments of reflective solitude where we can think through issues?*

What does freshness mean?

Freshness is about using our freedom in a creative way. How often do we:

- *try different ways of walking to work or involve ourselves in different community activities?*
- *try different types of food?*
- *consciously decide to experiment, using different words, different thought patterns and different approaches?*

It doesn't mean digging the garden with a spoon rather than a spade, but it might mean a different-shaped spade. Experimentation is not normally about doing something completely ridiculous (although sometimes it is). It is building on our understanding and trying to approach issues in a variety of different ways.

How radical should we be?

There are moments in time when we should be radical. There is a moment before choosing our life partner when we consciously make a major 'yes' or 'no' decision. When children leave home, there are big decisions that parents can make about life priorities. There may be a moment when we decide not to seek a life partner and to enjoy being single. Maybe we are too hesitant about being radical.

How open are you to radical decisions about:

- *your work choices?*
- *your pattern of activities during a typical week?*
- *your friendships?*
- *your time commitments?*

- *your political and religious beliefs?*

How frightening is freedom? How scared would you be if:

- *your job was coming to an end?*
- *your principal relationship was coming to an end?*
- *your children were at risk of taking decisions with which you are uncomfortable?*
- *your health was limiting some of your activities?*

For each of these areas of our life there may be a gloomy prognosis, and yet each could produce new freedoms that stretch our freedom of thought and our understanding of ourselves.

When you are frightened by freedom, how do you get it into proportion? Different approaches might be:

- *thinking hard into a situation about potential benefits;*
- *recognising how you have moved on in previous situations;*
- *celebrating small changes which have brought a freshness into your life.*

Great leaders have always stretched the boundaries of freedom. Moses led the children of Israel out of Egypt toward the Promised Land. Jesus encouraged his followers to be born again into a new way of living and thinking. Nelson Mandela, through his persistence and commitment, took 'the long road to freedom'. We admire those who have fought for freedom on our behalf. My wife's father would occasionally talk about taking part in the D-Day landings in Normandy. For him, the driver was the freedom he wanted to ensure for his children.

Freedom comes in many different shapes and sizes. I

travelled home on the train with Bill recently. It had just been agreed that he could retire early at 56. He was relishing the opportunity of doing more sailing and refurbishing his house near the sea. Freedom for him was following his own interests while recognising that his wife had a long list of practical tasks that he would be asked to do. In contrast, for Jim, freedom is about continuing to be able to work and bring his expertise as a quantity surveyor into a wide range of both work and charitable situations: at 68 the last thing he wants to do is retire.

For both Bill and Jim, what is important is the freedom to choose how they want to live their lives and contribute to others.

Moving on to new beginnings
Five key next steps on freedom:

- *Be clear about how much freedom you really want to have.*
- *How important is freedom of thought to you? How prepared are you to use that freedom? How are you going to take forward freedom of thought?*
- *Be specific about how you want to stretch the boundaries in the future.*
- *Articulate the key values that provide the framework for the way you are going to use your freedom.*
- *Set out the next steps you are going to take which will remove the fear out of freedom.*

Jennie's story
Jennie moved rapidly, doing a range of jobs. She was utterly single-minded but there were some shocks along the way: her

husband left her, there was a promotion but it did not work too well and she felt sidelined. Her particular approach at work ceased to be the flavour of the month.

Eventually she made a very bold decision and set up her own business. Within months she began to find her feet and made a great success of her consultancy work. She loved her new career freedom and her new home. She had made a major life-changing decision and her boldness had paid dividends, within the core framework of the importance of her children, her church, her home and her friends.

She had the courage to retain her freedom of thought, to consider other possibilities and to venture into new areas of life. The shocks along the way had been hard but her focus on using her freedom wisely worked well.

> *" Free at last! Free at last! Thank God Almighty, we are free at last! "*
>
> Martin Luther King

Chapter 12
FASTING

" The best of all medicines are resting and fasting. "
Benjamin Franklin

" One secret act of self-denial, one sacrifice of inclination to duty, is worth all the more good thoughts, warm feelings, passionate prayers in which idle people indulge themselves. "
John Henry Newman

What are our addictions? What is holding us back? Would self-denial or abstaining from particular things be helpful, or would it just add to life's frustrations? Might fasting, in a very broad sense of that word, help at key decision points? Is fasting a means of moving on?

What are we very dependent upon?

We have the luxury of owning two cars. One weekend both cars were away as two of the children had an essential need to use them, leaving us with no wheels! On the Saturday we walked the five miles from our home along the riverbank to Guildford, while on Sunday we walked to and from church and into the Surrey countryside. When the young people reappeared, we had not missed having a car at all: there was an odd sense of having had greater freedom resulting from walking everywhere and not having to look after the car.

When I walked the 108 miles across northern England from Arnside Pier to Saltburn Pier, there was something emancipating about having a rucksack containing all the possessions I needed for that week. I had cut down what I was carrying to an absolute minimum: one spare pair of trousers, one jumper, one pair of lightweight shoes. I was unencumbered and felt a great sense of freedom.

It is worth reflecting on what we are particularly dependent upon. Is it:

- *our car?*
- *our wardrobe?*
- *our computer?*
- *our televison?*
- *our mobile phone?*

Perhaps the biggest change in communications in recent years has been the introduction of the mobile phone. What a great asset that has been as a means of improving personal safety and communication. But it's been a mixed blessing, too, in terms of never being able to hide!

When we were on holiday in New England I could not resist having a quick look at the e-mails on my Blackberry. When we went up into the Vermont mountains the cell phone was not working. Oh dear, I couldn't look at the e-mails – oh good, I had a ready-made excuse for *not* looking at the e-mails!

It might be worth listing:

- *What are you most dependent upon?*

- *Can you imagine a world when you are not dependent upon these things?*
- *What would it be like to abstain from these things for a period?*
- *Would this be limiting or releasing?*

Abstaining from electronic communications

When I was Press Secretary to Kenneth Baker when he was a Cabinet minister, I used to buy all the Sunday newspapers and pick out the main themes. I was on call to journalists and to the Secretary of State. Frances insisted that the telephone was taken off the hook during Sunday lunch. No junior press officer or journalist was going to break into our family lunch. (I just hoped that Kenneth Baker was not trying to get through with an urgent request at the time!)

How good are we at drawing our boundaries in abstaining from modern communications?

- *E-mail is a wonderful way of keeping in touch, but do we define clearly when we are available and when we are not?*
- *The mobile phone can be so useful at particular moments, but do we keep it switched off enough?*
- *Texting can be great fun, but what would happen if we rationed ourselves to sending three text messages a day?*
- *The range of TV channels keeps us bang up to speed with world events, but what would happen if we limited ourselves to watching no more than half an hour per day?*

Limiting the amount of time that we spend closeted with electrical, electronic or IT equipment could provide us with a whole new realm of time to:

- *have one-to-one conversations;*
- *read books;*
- *begin to crystallise some of our thoughts rather than just produce instant reactions.*

The power of abstinence

On 1 December 1955 Rosa Parks refused to give up her seat on a bus in Alabama so that a white man could sit down. She was jailed and fined, and the Montgomery black community's pent-up resentment erupted. What started as a four-day bus boycott went on for more than a year. The boycott's leader, a little-known preacher called Martin Luther King Junior, was vaulted into national prominence and led the Civil Rights Movement to success a decade later. The black community's boycott of using the buses was a stand which led to the absurdity of racial segregation being brought into the public limelight: it set Martin Luther King on a pathway to his 'I have a dream' speech a few years later.

Boycotting the buses in Alabama created unstoppable change, as did boycotting goods from South Africa a couple of decades later. The more people buy fairly traded goods and abstain from buying goods where there is no assurance of fair trade, the stronger will be the impact on creating fairness in Third World economies.

Abstinence is something we might do for the benefit of others, but it also benefits us in limiting the way we are tied to particular material comforts or electronic aids. What might you abstain from? For example, might it be the TV, surfing the internet, excessive work, or shopping? This new available time might provide the opportunity to do more thinking, listening, encouraging and challenging.

It is worth reflecting on:

- *What might I do without today?*
- *What material things can I show to myself I am not dependent upon?*
- *How can I use the freedom which comes from being less dependent on certain things?*

Where does fasting from food and drink fit in?

There has been a remarkable change in custom and practice in the last few years about the consumption of alcohol. Every business lunch or all-day meeting used to include wine: those days are long gone. There was a sense of being frowned on if you did not drink alcohol: in most gatherings now, there is no surprise if some people only have soft drinks.

Fasting from certain foods has become a national pastime. There are a wide range of different carb-free diets: at one time in the USA up to 20 per cent of people were on the Atkins diet. It is fashionable to experiment with not eating certain types of food, with the results sometimes being spectacularly successful.

Fasting is not just a new fashion: it has always been present within the Judeo-Christian tradition. Although fasting may seem a thing of the past, there is still a custom of eating fish on Fridays in some households. Today young people may be more aware of fasting in different communities because of the greater emphasis in primary school education on understanding different religious traditions. Fasting may be less important nowadays in the Christian tradition but it is alive and well in the Jewish, Hindu and Muslim cultures. Fasting has also been used as a means of protest and to gain attention. Hunger strikes have been a powerful way of drawing attention to inequities.

When he was a teenager my eldest son and a number of his friends held a 24-hour sponsored fast outside a Sainsbury's supermarket to raise money for Soapbox, a charity working with children in Third World cities. To the considerable credit of Sainsbury's, the local manager was one of the sponsors for the fast. For these youngsters one of the pleasures of the fast was the feast they had at its conclusion!

Fasting in terms of food and drink can take many different forms. It could be:

- *no alcohol for a month;*
- *no red meat for a week;*
- *only fresh vegetables and fruit for a week.*

Ensuring a healthy intake is crucial but experimenting with fasting in different ways can make us feel healthier and make us feel more adaptable and flexible. It can be an effective way of preparing for life-changing decisions. As I made various big decisions just before I was 55, I lost nearly two stone of weight on the Atkins diet. That act of fasting was an important part of moving from one world into a very different sphere.

Is self-denial important or just another indulgence?

If self-denial makes us ratty or irritable, it may be time to think again. But if it gives us a greater sense of freedom, it might help us to make the best choices for the future. Denying ourselves a bigger house or an expensive suit or a new car may actually give us the freedom to use our time and resources in a very different way. The less dependent we are on satisfying our appetite for physical comfort, speed, communications, food and drink, the greater will be our freedom to make different choices, to spend quality time with those who are important to us and to stretch the boundaries of our thinking.

What if abstinence is really difficult?

Have you, like me, had a craving for chocolate when you are on a diet? We do not always succeed in abstinence. Fasting shows up our strengths and susceptibilities. The driver which provides our creativity is often the same driver which makes self-denial difficult. As we find our future, knowing and living with ourselves is part of our own journey of discovery. For each of us abstinence will come easily in some areas and not in others. Honesty and courage go hand in hand with living with ourselves.

Five practical tests when we feel a strong sense of dependency:

- *Is this addiction doing me any harm?*
- *What greater freedom would I have if I was less dependent on this addiction?*
- *How can I limit the scale of the addiction?*
- *What support will those around me give?*

- *What would I feel like if the dependency had gone away?*

Moving on to new beginnings

Five things to do about fasting:

- *Be clear about your levels of addiction or dependency.*
- *Decide which area you particularly want to tackle.*
- *Tell some good friends what you want to do to reduce the dependency.*
- *Decide on the rewards you might give yourself when you succeed.*
- *Recognise that you can only make progress one step at a time.*

Jack's story

Jack was a computer specialist who had lost his job. He was in his early thirties and was expected to get another job easily. But he withdrew into himself and spent his days surfing the net and playing computer games. As soon as he got up the computer was turned on: the new games were so lively, with always a new one to explore. His greatest friend was the laptop: he could not be separated from it as it gave him an enormous amount of pleasure. But he seemed to be losing the ability to have conversations and there was no incentive to make new friends, enjoy his work or develop his own independence. He and the laptop were so inseparable that nothing else seemed to matter.

One day, Jack's friends hid his laptop, forced him to go out for a walk and then sat with him at the local pub for a drink. They refused to give the laptop back to him until he had begun to talk with them about what steps he was going to take to get a job, how he was going to use his time in a different way and when he was going to cook himself a decent healthy meal. It was a real struggle for Jack to move on, and something was holding him back from using his considerable ability to best effect. But as he 'fasted' from the comfort blanket of his computer, he was able to begin to make progress. The 'fast' forced him to think clearly and helped him to see how his computer skills could be used to benefit new businesses. Ironically, it appeared that the thing he was good at was what he needed to be separated from in order to move forwards.

> *" I count him braver who overcomes his desires than him who overcomes his enemies. "*
>
> Aristotle

MOVING ON

In this final section we move from good intentions into action. Moving on is not about following whims or fashions. Moving on that is going to be permanent is likely to include:

- clear *foresight* looking five years ahead;
- a *focus* on key priorities;
- a strong sense of *fun* and seeing the lighter side;
- *fulfilment* that fully embraces what is important to us.

Sometimes moving on will mean spontaneous decisions, but more often next steps will result from careful thought. Trying to look ahead with foresight can provide a framework for our decisions. Being focused can help us discriminate between the more and the less important. A sense of fun is an essential prerequisite to being energised as we move forward. Looking for fulfilment that is consistent with our personal beliefs and values is necessary for our own peace of mind.

Moving on is about making decisions which stick while still being able to laugh at ourselves and our foibles. You will have reached a perspective on personal fulfilment that resonates with your fundamental values.

Chapter 13

FORESIGHT

" The empires of the future are the empires of the mind. "

Winston Churchill

" There is a time for everything, and a season for every activity under heaven: a time to be born and a time to die, a time to plant and a time to uproot. "

Ecclesiastes 3

How good are we at looking ahead? Does looking five years ahead excite us or depress us? Does looking ahead imply we are rushing our life away? How can we both be thinking ahead in a practical way and living each moment to its full? Is trying to have foresight an abdication of our current responsibilities or is it trying to take them forward in a positive way?

How well are we using our gifts?
Jim Houston was a senior lecturer in geography at Oxford University, where he had written a seminal work called *The Western Mediterranean World* and, as bursar of Hertford College, had built up skills in administration. His passion was in mentoring students and developing leadership skills: teaching geography at Oxford was only a partial use of his immense abilities.

After much heart-searching, at the age of 49 he became the Founding Principal of Regent College, Vancouver, which aimed to build a new generation of leaders open to new ideas and grounded in Christian understanding. The College grew from small beginnings to have a significant influence within North America. At the heart of Jim's impact has been his mentoring and nurturing of leadership based on the virtues of faith, hope and love. His gift for mentoring leaders was shaped by his experience at Oxford and had its fullest impact when he made this dramatic decision in his late forties to change jobs and continents.

A key starting-point in looking at our future is to be very clear about our gifts:

- *What do you think are the two main strengths which are your particular gifts?*
- *What do other people think are your gifts?*
- *How well have you been able to use those gifts so far?*
- *What is your dream about using those gifts effectively in the future?*

To what extent do we 'hide our light under a bushel'? If there is some activity which gives us the greatest joy, do we tend to ignore it, hide it or even suppress it? Why might this be? Your gift might be understanding people, building or being part of a team, pushing the boundaries, bringing creativity, turning a situation round, or helping to make change happen constructively.

How can you bring that gift to bear in a way which is going to have a long-term benefit both for yourself and for the organisations you are part of, in either an employed or a voluntary capacity?

Where do you want to be in five years' time?

The key starting-point must be realism. There will be major constraints, especially if:

- *you have a clear pathway for the education of your children;*
- *there are going to be aged parents who will need love and care;*
- *there are financial commitments which you do not want to reduce;*
- *there are obligations to your community, culture or faith which are of particular importance to you.*

Recognising the constraints of realism is not a sign of weakness. It is an acknowledgement of aspects of your life that are important to you and provide fixed points for your decision making. But within that framework, what are the freedoms that you want to explore? What are the areas where you can stretch the boundaries?

How might you be different in five years' time? This could cover:

- *your **employment**:*
- *will you be in a completely different type of job?*
- *your work **responsibilities**: will you have different responsibilities within a similar work environment?*
- *your **friendships**: have you made major decisions about which friendships you particularly want to grow?*
- *your **education**: is there an education programme or training course which you would like to do?*

- *your **physical fitness**: are there skills you want to develop or physical challenges you want to take on?*
- *your **emotional awareness**: are there psychology, counselling or self-awareness courses you would like to embark on?*
- *your **faith**: are there aspects of religious understanding you would like to explore further?*

Many of these different avenues can be explored within the framework of your current realities. It can be too easy to use the reality test as a reason for not exploring those avenues.

How flexible do you want to be?

A key issue is, how bold do you want to be in stretching the boundaries? A good way of testing this is to imagine yourself in different types of situations five years from now.

If one possible option might be to become:

- *a teacher: imagine what it is like to be in the classroom; what are the joys and the frustrations?*
- *a counsellor: what are the particular satisfactions and questions?*
- *a parent: what are the joys and sacrifices?*
- *a school or college governor: what are you contributing and learning?*
- *working with a local charity: what are the particular satisfactions and what reads across into other aspects of your life?*

Thinking hard about what it would feel like to be in a particular situation in five years' time can reinforce whether one route is the right direction of travel or somewhere you would prefer not to travel. This dreaming is not escapism but trying to build a clarity into whichever dream you want to pursue.

Martin Luther King said, 'I have a dream.' The dream of the end of segregation in the USA was fulfilled because people were clear about the vision they were aiming for and the next steps they wanted to take.

How bold do you want to be?

There are moments when it is right to take bold decisions or to set on a bold course. Sometimes a long lead time is necessary. Taking a degree course or a training course may take three years. But where the dream is strong and the passion to make progress is there, then the potentially unthinkable can happen. Even though the destination of a particular qualification or leadership role may seem a long way off, breaking the journey into manageable steps can produce a pathway that is attainable.

Last week I climbed the 298 steps to the top of the Bunker Hill Monument in Boston. In my unfit state I broke it up into chunks of 50 steps with a 5-second stop after each 100 steps. The rather depressing prospect of a long climb was turned into the great pleasure of looking at the skyline of Boston and the waters of the Atlantic. Chunked up, the climb became perfectly manageable.

This climb was an example to me of breaking up a challenge into smaller parts, making each part attainable and giving myself small rewards at each milestone.

The excitement of looking ahead

Foresight is not only about our own dreams; it is about thinking how the world will change over the next few years.

In five years:

- information technology will have been through another two revolutions;
- globalisation will have had dramatic effects on the way economies are organised;
- the children in our lives will be that much older;
- the nature and needs of the communities in which we live may have changed out of all recognition;
- further acts of terrorism by nations, groups or individuals may have created new suspicions or resulted in new alliances.

Some of the changes over the next five years are entirely predictable: we will all be five years older! Others will be less clear. Which changes in external factors do we hope will happen in the next five years? Which changes are we least prepared for? Which changes might help reinforce our dreams for five years on?

How prepared are we for risks and surprises? Whatever our dreams and however clearly we can plan a pathway, there will be risks and surprises.

Can we minimise the risks by:

- *eating wisely;*
- *keeping physically fit;*
- *not getting overtired through excessive work;*
- *ensuring healthy family life and friendships;*
- *keeping our emotional well-being in good shape through good self-awareness;*

- *ensuring a spiritual awareness that is rooted in a communion with others and not based on self-delusion.*

Whatever our dreams for the future, a key element is to be ready to be surprised. The walker determined to reach the top of a Scottish peak needs the resolve to keep going and the readiness to cope with surprises, which might range from slippery pathways to encircling clouds. Some of the surprises will be uncomfortable, particularly the howling gale, while others will be a source of encouragement: such as a shared conversation with those on a similar route.

If we set ourselves on a particular course, how best will we cope with adverse surprises? A strong sense of purpose and direction, the companionship of our friends, a strong sense of emotional resolve, belief in ourselves or a living out of our religious faith, can all be powerful tools in coping with adversity.

Foresight is not about knowing every answer. It is about being self-aware about your gifts and wanting to use them effectively. It is about the hard work of:

- *horizon scanning thoughtfully to build an awareness of your changing world and the part you would like to play;*
- *building some clarity about your next steps;*
- *being prepared to be surprised;*
- *being ready to take some risks.*

Foresight can sometimes be about looking through a glass darkly and seeing a broad shape of where you want to go. It would be all so predictable if the end point was crystal clear with no rocks on the way.

Moving on to new beginnings

Five practical steps on foresight:

- *Let yourself dream dreams.*
- *Consider how you could turn some of those dreams into reality.*
- *Decide which gifts you most want to build on.*
- *Be ready to be surprised.*
- *Be clear about who are your companions on the way and share your ideas with them.*

Darshan's story

Darshan had been very absorbed in his work in a big national organisation and had moved every two years to ever more difficult jobs. He liked the challenge of new responsibilities but it had begun to feel repetitive. Some of the joy had gone out of his work and he wanted to move on. He visualised working in a very different type of world which was much closer to individual customers. His previous work had been two steps away from 'real people'. He wanted to be closer to the problems that individuals faced in local communities.

He had huge analytic gifts and a wonderful way of getting alongside people and building partnerships. He decided to take the plunge and move to a very different sort of job in local government. In one sense it was a great risk, but rapidly his colleagues came to appreciate his particular gifts. One of his managers said, 'It's brilliant to have you around.' The danger was that people regarded him as the 'White Knight', but that was far better than being ignored! Darshan had had the foresight to see that his gifts were transferable and was so encouraged by his first steps into a very different world. He was still apprehensive but was well on his way to making an effective transition. He was so grateful that he had been bold enough to make this move. He was now seeing the practical differences he was able to make. The local community leaders were very grateful for what he had been able to do. He exuded energy and was ensuring that financial resources were being used much more effectively.

> *" Such a strong wish for wings. Such a thirst to see, to know, to learn. "*
>
> Charlotte Brontë

Chapter 14
FOCUS

" Always remember the future comes one day at a time. "

Dean Acheson

" The future is purchased by the present. "

Samuel Johnson

To what extent is life passing you by? Have there been opportunities that have come and gone? Have you had moments when you have been telling yourself to 'get a grip'? Are you focused enough in responding to the need for change and being clear about your own next steps?

How well are you using your energies?

In his book *It's Not About the Bike*, Lance Armstrong tells the remarkable story of his journey through cancer to win the first of his Tour de France victories. He says frankly that 'in an odd way, having cancer was easier than recovery'. After fighting the cancer with all the energy at his disposal, a clean bill of health brought a very different sort of problem. He wrote, 'I was a bum. I played golf every day, I water-skied, I drank beer, and I lay on the sofa and channel-surfed. I violated every rule of my training diet ... but it wasn't fun. It wasn't lighthearted or free or happy. It was forced. I was disorientated. Nothing was the same – and I couldn't handle it. I hated the bike.'

He commented that surviving cancer involved more than just a convalescence of the body; his mind and soul had to convalesce too. He needed those closest to him to understand him and recognise that these aspects of recovery were necessary too.

Training rides were no joy at all. His trainer persuaded him to ride Beech Mountain, a strenuous 5000-foot climb which had been the site of one of his former victories. As he struggled up the mountain he remembered the crowds that had lined the route and how they had painted across the road, 'Go Armstrong'. As he started up a tough rise he saw an eerie sight: the road still had his name painted on it. He rose out of his seat and picked up the pace. His trainer, Chris, rolled down the car window and began driving him on with 'Go, go, go! He wrote:

> *" That ascent triggered something in me. As I rode upwards, I reflected on my life, back to all points, my childhood, my early races, my illness, and how it changed me. Maybe it was the primitive act of climbing that made me confront the issues I'd been evading for weeks. It was time to quit stalling, I realised. 'Move', I tell myself, 'if you can still move you aren't sick'. "*

As he continued to the top, 'I saw my life as a whole. I saw the pattern and privilege of it, and the purpose of it, too. It was simply this: I was meant for a long hard climb.' His trainer saw in the attitude of his body on the bike that he was having a change of heart. Some weight, he sensed, was simply no longer there. That ride was the crucial point which renewed Armstrong's focus on becoming the best endurance cyclist in the world, leading to six successive Tour de France victories.

Our defining moments will seem very modest in contrast to Lance Armstrong's ride up Beech Mountain. Sometimes our defining moments are occasions of success and at other times they are moments of abject failure. Perhaps the most significant defining moments are when we begin to turn apparent failure into a new, more focused resolve. Because Armstrong's period of apathy was so acute, the ride up Beech Mountain was such a crucial point of renewal. There were many struggles ahead before he won the Tour de France, but his energies and will were now focused.

What is your nearest equivalent to Lance Armstrong's Beech Mountain climb?

- *What was your state of mind before the climb?*
- *Why were you in this 'slough of despond'?*
- *Who were the people alongside you who made the biggest difference?*
- *What did the experience renew in you?*
- *How were you different as a result of the experience?*

Building on success

Philip was in a very demanding international role where he had to chair a sequence of crucial meetings that were going to be much tougher than anything he had ever done before. He enjoyed the chairing. He had to build fresh alliances and try new approaches. His resolution was tested again and again. He talks of the calmness he felt in the most tense of negotiations.

He didn't know he had it in him. There was a sweet joy of success following three very tough months. He now knew that he could handle successfully the toughest of negotiations and keep an inner calm.

Building on your successes is a crucial way of focusing your energies:

- *What have been your crucial successes over the last year?*
- *What did you learn about yourself from those successes?*
- *How can you build on those skills that proved successful?*
- *What are your next steps in taking forward these successful skills?*

Where do you want to make the biggest impact?

Focus is about making choices. When Lance Armstrong climbed Beech Mountain, he made a choice, to the great relief of his trainer.

When looking forward, key issues are:

- *Are you clear about where you would like your key focus to be over the next year?*
- *If it is unclear, what is the best way for you to clarify that focus?*
- *Who are the two or three significant others who can help you work through that focus?*
- *How will you know when you have got a clarity of focus?*
- *How will you celebrate that moment with your significant others?*

How well are you prioritising your time?

Focus is not about doing one thing to the exclusion of every-thing else: it is about using our time and energy as efficiently as we can. Some of the most influential people I have met have deliberately not devoted 24 hours a day, seven days a week to one purpose. They have used their time in a highly effective way, juggling a whole sequence of responsibilities. If we are trying to spin too many plates at the same time, some are bound to crash. But spinning just a few plates at the same time keeps us alert, enabling us to transfer the skill of spinning a soup bowl into the best way of spinning a dessert plate.

Key questions are:

- *How many plates are we trying to spin at the same time?*
- *Can we reduce the number of plates?*
- *If we want to add a plate, what else is going to give?*
- *Are we transferring our learning from spinning one plate into spinning another?*

Key reflections might be:

- *How well do I balance my different priorities?*
- *Are there radical changes I need to make in terms of dropping priorities?*
- *How can I move on and not let people down?*
- *What are the practical steps I now need to take?*

It can be very hard to stop doing certain tasks. Moving on can bring a sense of letting people down or not contributing where we think we have something to offer. But moving on gives other people opportunities and allows us to use our gifts in new ways in different places with different people.

Receiving feedback as a gift

Gus O'Donnell, Cabinet Secretary and Head of the UK Civil Service, talks of feedback as the biggest gift you can give anyone. We can too easily travel on a particular route blinkered to the impact we are having on those around us. They may be seething with fury or utterly dejected by our attitude and we fail to notice. Such insensitivity is perhaps the most gross act of selfishness by any manager.

Quality feedback can come through:

- *observing people's reactions to what we do or say: what seems to energise them or depress them;*
- *asking those closest to you for honest feedback;*
- *inviting an independent person such as a coach or mentor to give their impartial views;*
- *inviting the key people around you to give their impartial views to a friend or coach who can then feed these back to you in an anonymised way.*

Using feedback effectively can be a powerful way of deciding how we want to recreate ourselves and refocus the impact we want to have on others. Done badly, this process can be very destructive. Done well, it can continually refresh and renew how we impact on others.

Effective self-awareness is such an important gift. Caroline was very clear with her friend, William, that when he gave a presentation at an interview he should stick to the ten-minute maximum time set out in the brief. William brushed this

---

advice aside, saying, 'Of course, but if I am to be spontaneous I cannot over-prepare.' The chairman of the panel had to bring his presentation to an end after 20 minutes. There was no chance that William was going to be appointed. He just did not listen and failed to follow basic advice from his friend. Sometimes asking a friend the very basic question, 'What is the most significant way in which I can focus my contribution?' can lead to very simple, clear feedback. It is well worth continually asking this open question and being ready to listen to whatever is the answer.

How open are we to refocusing?

A key question is, how prepared are we to refocus? The apostle Paul, on the road to Damascus, turned his focus through 180 degrees. Instead of leading the persecution of the embryonic Christian Church, he became one of its leaders. This refocusing was not a sign of weakness but of strength. Sometimes effective refocusing knows no boundaries. On other occasions, the refocusing is within clear boundaries determined by our beliefs, our values, our financial commitments and our family responsibilities.

Moving on to new beginnings

Five practical steps:

- *What are your equivalent stories to the Beech Mountain ride?*
- *How strong is your need and will to refocus?*
- *What refocusing are you now going to do?*
- *Can you get more feedback from others to help you refocus?*
- *Are there obstacles you can remove?*

Sarah's story

Sarah prized herself on her independence and did a sequence of jobs in a single-minded way. She fell out of favour with her bosses because she didn't always listen to what they said: perhaps she began to try too hard and the situation got worse rather than better. Through no fault of her own, some of the projects she was involved in were less successful than had been expected.

After talking it through with close friends and hidden spells of anger and tears, she completely changed her focus and moved to a very different type of work environment, where she recreated herself. She built up her clarity of thinking and determination, but there was now more of a lightness of touch and more joy. She had refocused both the type of work she did and her approach. The result was both more fulfilment in her work and a renewed level of personal fulfilment.

> " *I was no longer the angry and unsettled young rider I had been. My racing was still intense, but it had become subtler in style and technique, not as visibly aggressive. Something different fuelled me now – psychologically, physically and emotionally – and that something was the Tour de France.* "
>
> Lance Armstrong, seven-times winner of
> the Tour de France

Chapter 15

FUN

" Laugh, and the world laughs with you. Weep, and you weep alone. "

Ella Wheeler Wilcox

" Nothing like a little judicious levity. "

Robert Louis Stevenson

There is nothing so deadly as a boring meeting with no laughter and no sense of fun. Our survival in so many spheres depends on a shared sense of humour, the ability to bring a light touch and the opportunity to relax amidst busy and stressful situations. A shared sense of fun or ritual is crucial for any team that is going to survive and be adaptable. A sense of fun is not an optional extra.

Are we sometimes too serious for our own good?

John was getting more and more concerned about a decision he had to make: should he stay teaching in his present school or should he accept a job in another town? As he wrestled with this decision he became more and more stuck in the mire. There was no lightness left; either option seemed full of problems. The joy had gone out of the decision. What should have been an exciting reflective moment became almost one of despair.

He tried to think of the benefits of staying where he was: enjoying the young people and staff he knew. There were also the benefits of moving elsewhere, including more opportunities to be creative. Should he stay in a place which he might tire of, or should he go to a different place where he was unsure how well he would cope? He worried away at this dilemma and could not get it out of his mind.

The person who made all the difference was Sunil, who got him to think about what he would enjoy most about the new job and what he would enjoy most if he stayed in his current role. What would make him smile most in a different school? What would he laugh about most if he stayed in his current role? As John's spirits lifted, the agony of the choice became the quiet consideration of two rather good alternatives. The more positively he felt about those options, the more he was gradually drawn towards accepting the offer of a new job. When the conversation with his friend ended, he moved on with a spring in his step and a contentment about his decision.

When it comes to big decisions, it is worth being dispassionate about what drags us down and what helps lighten our spirit. Drawing lessons from our past experience is a clear starting-point:

When you have had difficult decisions to make in the past:

- *What has helped you reach a conclusion?*
- *How have you been able to smile about the alternatives?*
- *Who have you been able to laugh with as you have reflected on different alternatives?*

- *What helped you relax in making those decisions?*

Using humour as a facilitator

Hilary hated going to drinks parties or other networking events. She was unsettled by needing to talk to so many people. Starting a conversation was bad enough, but ending it politely was even more difficult! She avoided these events but knew that they were very important to her in her job. She decided to turn these events into a bit of a game. She challenged herself to talk to ten people in half an hour. She made a mental list that she was going to talk to the tallest person, someone in a red tie, an individual in the worst-cut suit and whoever was wearing the ugliest glasses. In this way she overcame her nerves and was able to talk to a wide range of people. It even meant that moving on from a conversation became much easier, as there was a natural glint in her eye as she said goodbye.

When people are nervous about going into a major interview I encourage them to try and view the situation in a way that will make them smile. I encouraged someone who was very nervous to imagine the interviewers wearing pantomime outfits. If you are imagining the rather severe Chair of a panel dressed up as Little Bo-Peep, you can hardly but smile at the most serious of questions! This may sound rather trivial. But the more we can smile at ourselves, the more we will smile at others and the more they will be relaxed in our company.

A senior manager once told me that my effect as a coach on her staff was that they had become more focused and relaxed at the same time. That, to me, is what enabling someone to grow into any job is about. It is a clear focus on what is most important coupled with a relaxation and a sense of fun that helps bring other people on-side.

But is fun falseness?

There is nothing worse than the superficial joke or the teasing comment which completely misses the mark. There are few things more grating than having to fake a smile after the attempted joke by the Chair of a meeting. Using humour effectively demands careful skill. But it can be learnt.

The starting-point is what makes you smile. Is it:

- *a sense of the absurd?*
- *the pleasure of a shared endeavour?*
- *the glint in someone's eyes?*
- *the sense of what might have happened if the wall had fallen in?*

As you reflect on what makes you smile, focus on that before you go into a difficult meeting or make a difficult decision. That will help you get your thinking into proportion. Using humour successfully can be practised in a similar way to other skills. It is worth experimenting, but in a way that is true to yourself. Always be ready to share the joke and talk through the funny side of different situations. The sense of the ridiculous can keep us going in the most demanding of contexts. It will lighten your spirit and also the spirits of those with whom you are working.

What is the link between fun and relaxation?

As we think about different options for our own future, we will be thinking clearly both about the skills we will be able to use and the extent to which we will enjoy those different options. The more we are able to enjoy different alternatives, the more we will feel relaxed and the more effective will be our contribution. Sometimes the choices do not seem to involve a great deal of joy. It is either staying at home looking after the children or seeking a part-time job which will be more tiring but will create a little extra income. Seeing some element of joy that might result from this decision is crucial to making a good decision and one we will be able to stick with.

The absence of joy as an indicator

If there is no sense of joy in the work you do, if you wake up at four o'clock in the morning worrying about going to work, then maybe it is time to think again and possibly move on. How do you balance staying in a well-paid job against the way that job might eat away at the sense of joy in your life? Roger had come to hate the work he did. It was pure drudgery and the commuting was getting him down. He arrived home energyless and was no good for anything else. At last he resigned: the first reaction was ecstasy and two weeks later depression, as he began to think about what he was going to do next. He found a new role, paying two-thirds of his original salary, but he was at home more, relaxed and enjoying life much more. The financial sacrifice was as nothing compared to finding himself again and smiling with his eyes rather than through clenched teeth.

Stephen was taking himself far too seriously. He could not laugh at himself. He began to be unable to see the good and the creative in other people. He looked stressed and there was no lightness in his eyes. He began to work harder and harder and feel less and less fulfilled. His best friend took him aside and told him to stop working so hard and to ensure that he relished those things outside his work that he enjoyed the most. He began to have a glass of red wine again and began to run again. He allowed his friends to tease him again. At last he began to loosen up. His decisions became easier to make. He carried people with him more effectively. He was ready to move on.

For both Roger and Stephen there was a moving on when they were willing to tackle the absence of joy in their working lives. Only when they were willing to face up to this reality could they make progress.

Seeking out fun

Cherishing moments of fun with our family and friends is one of the most precious things we can do. If your family enjoy raspberry ripple ice-cream, enjoy it together as often as you reasonably can. If barn dancing is something that you get a lot of enjoyment from, find the best possible barn dance to which you can invite your friends.

As we indulge in moments of fun we rediscover ourselves, our friendships and our own sense of well-being. We create situations and experiences which equip us in the best possible way for making important decisions about our future.

What helps you to smile most? Is it:

- *your family?*
- *your friends?*
- *familiar situations?*
- *very different situations?*
- *your favourite comedian?*
- *re-watching videos that make you laugh the most?*

Whatever makes you laugh, put yourself in that situation on a regular basis.

Moving on to new beginnings

Five ways to reinforce a sense of fun:

- *Always look for the absurd in any situation.*
- *Try smiling and see what other people do.*
- *Bring in a lighter touch to try and gently steer a discussion.*
- *Relive your most joyful moments before making difficult decisions.*
- *Make relaxation a high priority.*

Julia's story

Julia was a tough and determined lady who was always thorough in the work she did. She worked hard but also thoroughly enjoyed her life at home with her husband. She hated pretence and always brought a strong sense of Northern realism.

Her greatest gift was that she could make the boss laugh. However tense the situation, she had this remarkable gift of defusing it. When the work was done she was the first to produce a bottle of wine. She could see the funny side in any situation. She helped people relax: they opened up with her. She had them eating out of her hands, be it the boss, a demanding colleague, an important client or the most junior member of staff. Humour well timed and well chosen was the glue she used to build a strong sense of common purpose. It was a remarkable gift which helped her shape the future in one organisation after another. Many people were grateful to her for that humour which helped them move on to new spheres, encouraged by her laughter, her teasing and that glass of red wine.

" It is a splendid thing to laugh at yourself. It is the best way of regaining your good humour and of finding God without further anxiety. "

Henri de Tourville

Chapter 16

FULFILMENT

" The future is something which everyone reaches at the rate of 60 minutes an hour, whatever he does, whoever he is. "

C. S. Lewis

" Let us, then, be up and doing
With a heart for any fate;
Still achieving, still pursuing,
Learn to labour, and to wait. "

Henry Wadworth Longfellow

What is a fulfilled life? Where does success fit in? Is success part of fulfilment or a distortion of it? Is seeking fulfilment looking for false horizons and not living enough in the present? How can we both enjoy the present to the full and also be on a journey where we are seeking to make a difference? Where does hope fit in: is that just a denial of the importance of living in the present? What aspects of fulfilment are most important to us?

What are our greatest moments of fulfilment?
Fulfilment comes in many different shapes and sizes. Chris does the night shift on the reception desk at a hotel in Boston.

He talks knowledgeably about American life and politics and knows a great deal about the sights and people of Boston. The job provides the sort of fulfilment he wants – a stress-free environment. He likes working through the night talking to the guests who appear, like me, for a chat at 6 a.m. For him fulfilment is ensuring the hotel is a secure and welcoming place in the early hours. Chris is clearly intelligent and able: he could do a job which is much more demanding. But he is fulfilled where he is, so why should he be pressured to do something which is a lot more stressful?

As you observe the people you meet, what do you think provides fulfilment for the cheerful waitress in the coffee bar, the postman who delivers your mail, the ticket inspector who checks your rail pass, or the policeman who is observing the busy crowd?

Fulfilment is often about:
- a job well done, whatever it is;
- making a difference, however big or small that difference is;
- keeping a regular flow of income to pay for food and shelter;
- sharing love and affection with at least one person;
- enjoying the respect and trust of those around you.

Can you define what aspects of fulfilment are most important to you in:

- *your family life?*
- *your friendship world?*
- *your community?*
- *your work world?*

- *your personal learning?*
- *your self-awareness or faith journey?*

Who are your role models?

As a teenager growing up in Yorkshire, one of the most significant influences on me was a lady in her nineties. She had a weak heart and hardly went out of her house. She had been a vicar's wife in the inner suburbs of London before they moved to a Sheffield steel-manufacturing district. When her husband died she was left with no home; her second husband also died, as did her third. She had not been able to have children. In one sense there was no fulfilment: no children, three husbands who predeceased her and very poor health. But there was a richness of experience, a generosity of spirit, an openness of thought and a liveliness of faith. She fully engaged me in conversation, entering into my world in a way that was enriching and challenging. She was one of the most fulfilled people I have ever met. There was an inner contentment that enabled her to cope with her health troubles. She could have been full of sadness. The opposite was the case because she celebrated the good moments and saw the sad moments in a very reflective light.

Whatever our age, it is worth reflecting on those we know whom we regard as the most fulfilled. It may well not be a fulfilment measured in pounds or dollars or in the opulence of their clothes or lifestyle. The fulfilment may be more reflected in a twinkle in the eye or in the pleasure of being in their company.

A crucial test is what happens to you when you are one-to-one with important people in your life. In the privacy of that conversation, do they unnerve you, alienate you, challenge you or encourage you? If a consequence of that one-to-one engagement is that you are encouraged, you are embracing into yourself some of the fulfilment of the other person. Perhaps the most fulfilling thing for each of us as individuals is to spend time one-to-one with family, friends and colleagues so that part of our sense of fulfilment is passed on to others in a way that builds hope and not envy. We all need role models. They are not an optional extra. They do not need to be rich or famous but they do need, in some way, to be people who are fulfilled.

Enjoy fulfilment

Often we are bad at enjoying special moments in our lives. Some of the most fulfilled moments for me have included a barn dance with our friends when Frances and I reached the age of 50; going on the Millennium Wheel in London with my family after receiving the CB from the Queen; and a meal together as a family after our younger two children had received the Duke of Edinburgh Gold Award. Fulfilment was about celebrating with family and friends and standing still long enough to enjoy that sense of fulfilment.

The heart of fulfilment is about what we do with our family and friends at key moments in our lives and not about our jobs and careers. Do we give ourselves enough time for this? It is never too late to start, if we feel that we have not done enough of this in the past.

Fulfilment may be about doing something completely different. Is there something you have always wanted to do, and now might be the moment to do it? For many years I had wanted to walk across England. When our children were young this would have been a completely unrealistic or selfish way of using a week's holiday. But eventually, with the strong support of my family, I decided to walk from Arnside Pier in

Cumbria to Saltburn Pier in North Yorkshire. My daughter walked the first day with me. On seven of the nine days I had companions, including a friend from my undergraduate days, a friend from my postgraduate days, the father of one of my eldest son's friends, a friend from my Durham days and a new work colleague. My companions were my life in microcosm. Nothing could be more fulfilling than walking down Saltburn Pier and holding the metal railings at the end with the fresh and salty air blowing on my face. For me, this was the most fulfilling moment you could possibly imagine.

What is the equivalent sort of fulfilling moment that would be most special to you? This is not about selfish indulgence. It is about bringing together some of your friends and life experiences so that you can move on in a new way to cope with different challenges in your life. The last day of my walk across England was my fifty-fifth birthday: it was my transition into a very different world of executive coaching. I had exchanged managing groups of up to 900 staff for working with individuals and groups to help them develop their management skills. My fulfilment was enabling others to fulfil themselves. My new role was not only to help them be successful but also to enable them to find what would be their most important sources of fulfilment. What was going to be their equivalent of the walk across England? What would be their Saltburn Pier experience?

Fulfilment is not winning every battle

The turning-point in the American War of Independence was the Battle of Bunker Hill in June 1775. The British Regulars faced a motley collection of Colonial Militia who built a temporary fort on the top of a shallow hill overlooking Boston Harbour. The British forces were confident about quelling this insurrection: the highly trained Redcoats tried to storm the fort. The Colonials waited until they saw the 'whites of the Redcoats' eyes' and repelled the British twice. Eventually the Redcoats did storm the fort, but at a terrible cost. Of the 2000 Redcoat soldiers engaged, there were over 1000 casualties. More officers were killed than in any other battle in the war. Although the Redcoats won the battle, they were devastated by the scale of the casualties. The Americans saw that maybe with the resolve shown at Bunker Hill, they could win the war.

A fulfilled life is full of battles that have been lost. Looking back, perhaps some of the main defining moments have been the relationship that ended in tears, the essay that was full of red lines, the project which failed, or the task that just would not come to the right conclusion. Fulfilment is so often dependent on how we respond to adverse circumstances.

When things go wrong.

- *How do we cope with the sense of failure?*
- *What do we do with our resentment?*
- *Can we turn the anger into new energy?*
- *How can we build effectively on the learning that we have gone through?*

Creating long-term fulfilment is about:

- *allowing ourselves to be resurrected after each time we have felt knocked or damaged;*
- *allowing 'hope to spring eternal' by seeing each incident as a step on our pathway and not an end in itself;*
- *enjoying our defining moments and spending enough time in*

them to embrace the moment;

- *accepting that while we may lose individual battles, it is all about 'winning an overall war';*
- *allowing ourselves to continue to grow in terms of emotional and spiritual understanding.*

We will never be fulfilled in every area of our lives. To expect 'success' in every aspect of our family, friendship, community, work, intellectual, physical, emotional and spiritual lives is unrealistic. There will be moments of great sadness, grief, failure, regret and rejection. Fulfilment is about the way we accept and enjoy success but also how we live through the bad times.

Living with ambiguity is unavoidable. There will always be the tension of what might have been. There will always be emotional drivers that we cannot fulfil. We often have to accept second best in different spheres of our lives. That does not mean failure. It is in the way that we live with ambiguity that we can experience the greatest sense of fulfilment. It is in these moments that we accept the mix of who we are and we are honest with ourselves and – for those with religious faith – with our God.

Fulfilment is following that dream

Fulfilment is about wanting to make a difference in the areas that are most important to you. It is about hard prioritising and being determined to move forward with firm footsteps on your journey.

If fulfilment is about:

- *building a strong, loving family;*

- *creating an enduring network of friends;*
- *making a big difference in your chosen work environment;*
- *building a strong sense of community in your voluntary activities;*
- *developing your intellectual, emotional and spiritual understanding –*

then go for it!

If, having thought carefully about the impact on others, your fulfilment is about walking across England, then try to find the opportunity to do it. If it is about climbing a particular mountain in your life, then do it. If it is about reinventing yourself in a particular way to take account of changed circumstances, then seriously look at whether this is possible.

The greatest religious and political leaders have encouraged the renewal of energy in their followers, and have created in them a self-belief which is about enabling and not destroying others, about creating new horizons, about building love and not hate. A fulfilment based on 'loving others as yourself'.

The best sort of fulfilment is bringing enrichment, hope and joy to those around us. It is helping to transform lives. Finding your future is about enabling others to find their future.

Moving on to new beginnings

Five key steps about fulfilment:

- *Be clear about in which aspects of your life fulfilment is most important.*
- *Who are your role models about a fulfilled life?*
- *Within the test of realism, how much scope is there for more*

fulfilment in areas that are important to you?

- *What are your preferred next steps?*
- *Can you bring on board the people who are most important to you?*

Penny's story

Penny had done all the right jobs. She had been a counsellor, a manager and a teacher, and she attached great importance to professional fulfilment. But her husband was having a tough time in his work and her kids were a bit unsettled in their teenage years. She decided not to apply for one particularly demanding opportunity. It would have been a valuable promotion but she put her family first and decided to stay where she was. At first she thought people would think her a failure for not applying.

She thought that she would feel disappointed by her decision, but there was a sense of relief that at last she had got her priorities in balance. Yes, she would miss the challenge of this job, but there was so much she could do to make a big difference in her current role. There was much scope for fulfilment, whilst preserving all that was so important in her family life. She thought through much more clearly what fulfilment meant in different areas of her life. She became much calmer in setting out what really mattered to her and what was secondary. Penny became a superb adviser to others because of the journey she had travelled through.

> *" How much better to get wisdom than gold, to choose understanding rather than silver. "*
>
> Proverbs chapter 16

LIVING HOPEFULLY

Thank you for your perseverance in reading to the end. I hope there has been some resonance with your own experience. Engage with whichever one of the 16 chapter titles resonates for you. Think about the word from different angles. Why is it important to you? What does it echo from your own experience? Does it help you in some small way to find your own future?

Finding your future is not about reckless acts which are not rooted in realism. It is about being very clear concerning the constraints upon you and your obligations to others. Then it is being bold and setting off on the next step of your life's journey, determined to make a difference in your chosen sphere and to provide a source of encouragement and challenge both for those you love and for other fellow travellers in different aspects of your life.

My final plea to you, the reader, is that you believe that renewal and resurrection are possible both in your life and in the lives of others. Never give up hope of transformation. We have the capacity for new birth, new ideas, new experiences and discovering new qualities in ourselves. Be realistic but also be relentless in taking yourself into new horizons. When you are fit, may there be new mountains of discovery. When you are much more restricted, may there be new conversations or the renewal of old friendships.

Above all, never give up hope in yourself and others.

" Be joyful in hope, patient in affliction, faithful in prayer ... Do not be overcome by evil; but overcome evil with good. "

Romans 12